Manage IT!

Manage IT!

Exploiting information systems
for effective management

Michael Wright and
David Rhodes

PRAEGER SPECIAL STUDIES • PRAEGER SCIENTIFIC

New York • Philadelphia • Eastbourne, UK
Toronto • Hong Kong • Tokyo • Sydney

Published in the United States in 1986 by Praeger Publishers
CBS Educational and Professional Publishing
a Division of CBS Inc.
521 Fifth Avenue, New York, NY 10175 USA

Published in Great Britain in 1985 by Frances Pinter (Publishers) Limited

6789 000 987654321

Printed in Great Britain

Library of Congress Cataloging-in-Publication Data
Wright, Michael, 1952–
    Manage it!
    Includes index.
    1. Management—Data processing.   I. Rhodes, David.
II. Title.
HD30.2.W75   1985   658 '.05   85-28114
ISBN 0-03-008344-3

Contents

Preface

The emphasis in most discussion of Information Technology (IT) to date has focused on the relative capabilities of the myriad of hardware and software involved. There is a sad delusion that as long as the IT works technically and reliably the system is a success. So it may be on one level. But there may also be serious problems in that the recently acquired IT may not really be doing the job it was supposed to do, that the job is the wrong one in the first place, and that employees in the organization may be by-passing the system for one reason or another. These are essentially problems concerned with the management of the introduction of IT. Such problems have tended to be ignored or at least trivialized. Part of the reason is probably that many of those involved with the introduction of IT in companies are perhaps interested in the more precise area of computing rather than in the more nebulous area of management. A second reason lies in the perspective of managers who believe, or who are led to believe, that IT is the answer to all their problems without understanding its implications. It is to try and rectify what we see as an imbalance that we have written this book.

The work from which this book is drawn is based on the collaborative efforts of two authors from very different disciplines. One of us, David Rhodes, is by background an electrical engineer, whilst the other, Mike Wright, is an industrial economist and accountant. That it took at least a year before each understood what the other was saying illustrates the problem of integrating different approaches, which is a major theme of the book.

In writing the book we have benefited greatly from

discussions with colleagues, fellow academics, managers and employees in a variety of organizations. Particular thanks for helpful insights go to Gerry Waterlow, Maurice Bonney, and Charles Snyder. Grateful thanks are also extended to the managers and employees in the organizations which appear in the case studies.

Christine Waddon and Louise Wallace are to be commended for their ability to convert our manuscript into and out of electronic signals on a floppy disc. We acknowledge also the Institution of Electrical Engineers for providing several of the examples in Chapter 8.

1 Introduction

A report in *Fortune* in September 1982 estimated that over 60 per cent of microcomputers sold in American stores were purchased for business use. However, many purchasers were unable to make full use of the machines' capabilities because of their lack of expertise. An earlier study by the International Machine Tool Task Force published in 1980 and sponsored jointly by the US Airforce and the Society of Manufacturing Engineers demonstrated that the low utilization rates of machine tools was primarily due to poor management and organizational problems. On a wider front, a 1982 survey in the United Kingdom, indicated that more than 80 per cent of the population had heard of IT (Information Technology), but what they actually understood by the term was not established. However in 1985 a Mori Poll found that only 43 per cent of a sample of 1,824 interviewees did understand the term.

This evidence, from different quarters, illustrates the problem that, despite a high level of awareness of IT and enthusiasm for it, in reality IT is poorly perceived. Obtaining the best results from IT goes far beyond anything to do with the capabilities of the technology itself. Education in technology must come before an explanation, but the technical facts are only a small part of the story. Although the survey results just quoted are now dated, the problem that they highlight is still with us. There are still very few accounts of how people and IT might learn to co-exist, of where the fundamental opportunities and difficulties lie, or of how and when to innovate. Most writing is about 'high-tech' products for a particular purpose. The 'ways and means' of assimilating change are sadly neglected, and it is to this aspect of IT that the book addresses itself. The ways and means of assimilating change are in practice usually very narrowly defined. As one researcher in the area has remarked:

> "Most organisations believe that they have successfully implemented new operating technology when two conditions are met. First, when all the bugs have been ironed out and that it is working technically. Second, when the operation is working reliably ... however, when you probe beneath the surface, one must question the success of 'successful systems'."

Drawing on case studies carried out in the United Kingdom, United States and Australia, Voss (1985) concludes that the weight of evidence indicates that failure to realize the full benefits of new manufacturing technologies occurs principally because they are managed in traditional ways which are inappropriate, because there is a failure to manage the learning process and because there is a failure to manage the work-force appropriately. Although Voss was referring specifically to new manufacturing technologies, the problems he highlights are relevant to IT generally, since a Mori poll in 1982 showed that 90 per cent of businessmen thought IT would make their company more productive and competitive.

In developing an approach to how to introduce IT it is necessary first to understand what is meant by IT, and secondly why a firm should seek to introduce it.

What is IT?

Information technology is a recent term used to describe any equipment or mechanism involved in the processing, storage, display or communication of information or data. Its importance is perhaps less in the definition, which is reasonably obvious, than in the fact that such a word is important enough to be added to the general vocabulary. Papyrus, clay tablets, quill pens and ink are examples of IT, so too are signal flags and semaphore. Between them they cover the aspects referred to above of storing, displaying and communicating. Writing both stores and displays, flags display and communicate. In terms of quantity, writing, for example, stores typically 350 words per page or tablet, and Nelson's flags, with the help of an extensive book of reference codes, can convey a few sentences per hour. By today's standards, they are a poor means of communication, and contain little evidence of the other ingredient of IT, that is, processing power.

In stark contrast, modern IT is revolutionary. It has considerable processing power, independent of human intervention. This was created by the invention of the transistor in 1948 and the subsequent development of manufacturing processes which permit many such devices to be assembled on a single chip of semiconductor, typically in excess of 20,000 per square centimetre. The processing ideas already developed theoretically and evident to some extent in large, costly and mostly unreliable equipment containing electronic valves were, at the time of these inventions, available for immediate exploitation. This gave impetus to the revolution because the new technology was not only several orders of magnitude smaller but also cheaper and more reliable. The increased market for electronics goods also brought competition and economies of scale to reduce costs and price further. But, revolutionary though the effects may be, they are consistent with normal technical developments, well illustrated in history. Semaphore became the telegraph when electricity was used to transmit one piece of information by wire. The telegraph evolved progressively into the telephone, radio, radar, television, satellite communications and cable television as improvements in the theory of electromagnetic radiation were supported by better and cheaper equipment with more and more processing power. A laser printer can read, process and print

20,000 characters per second, while a television screen displays approximately a million items of information every 1/50th of a second. Each item is processed in that time by the camera, transmitter, receiver and screen!

Modern computers are practical achievements with dramatic improvements (Table 1.1). The ideas of Babbage, Turing and Von Neumann, on which they are based, have been around for a long time, so the recent success is due to the computer being both a cheap and effective solution. Initially, integrated circuits made the microcomputers possible, but recently the development of reliable disc drives to store information at relatively low cost (10 Mbytes per £1,000) has been a more important factor.

Table 1.1 Twenty-five years of computer engineering: a comparison

Year	1959	1984
Machine	Pegasus	ICL personal computer
Status	Medium performance/cost (smaller of a range of two)	Low performance/cost (smallest of range)
Price	£750,000 approx., 1984 prices	From £2,000
Central processor	375 packages	1 card
Working store	105 packages = 1000 bytes	1 card = 250,000 bytes
Permanent store	Magnetic drum = 42,000 bytes Magnetic tape = 100,000 bytes (12 in diameter + 0.5 in)	5¼ in floppy disc =500,000 bytes
Preventive maintenance	Check all components every 2 years	None needed
Engineering support	1 engineer resident, half-time	Take it to a service centre
Typical environment	Air-conditioned computer room	Desktop anywhere
Performance	3000 instructions per second	1 million instructions per second
Power consumption	13.5 kW	280 W
Weight	900 kg	16 kg
Number sold	40	Thousands

Source: J. M. Watson, 'The Technology that Makes IT Possible', *Electronics and Power* (house journal of the Institution of Electrical Engineers), January 1985, p. 15.

There are other areas of mechanical rather than electronic achievement. Most printers can produce at least as many lines a second as a typist can produce words, and some printers can produce as many pages. There are also the ubiquitous copying machines and many thousands of machine tools which, instead of being worked by hand, are controlled by programs. This is a very significant point. Not only are computers powerful processors (hardware) but through the use of programs (software) that processing power may be used very flexibly. In this way the same computer can be used for a wide variety of tasks. Software is crucially important; its value is in the flexibility it brings to processing power. Modern telephone exchanges, for example, are computers with programs to control the interconnections and flow of calls. They are no longer buildings full of switches. Without software IT might not exist. It would certainly be a pale shadow of its current self.

Why IT?

The research by Voss, quoted earlier, suggests that a typical rationale for the introduction of IT goes something like 'We have a (fill in blank space) problem, computers are used for solving (fill in blank space) problems, therefore we shall buy a computer and solve our (fill in blank space) problem'. This kind of statement is reminiscent of those heard some years ago when main-frame computers were first introduced. It seems a lot has been learned on the technical side, but not much from the managerial point of view.

In essence, the question 'Why IT?' really leads right back to what the business is about. To some extent, commercial organizations are about surviving in a competitive, changing environment. The first role of IT is, therefore, in contributing to the firm's ability to remain in business in such circumstances. An excellent example of the way in which IT can make a substantial contribution to competitiveness emerges from a comparison of the experiences of regional and national newspapers in the United Kingdom.

A provincial newspaper, the *Nottingham Evening Post*, installed the most modern equipment available in 1974 and has continued to keep it up-to-date. There are ten editions of the paper per day and the company also produces weekly papers for eleven other towns. The type-setting and text-editing equipment is under-utilized, and the company thus does a large amount of sub-contract work with little additional overhead. The company is profitable, a business success and well-known nationally.

In London, to the present day, *The Times* and several other famous newspapers are prepared and printed with obsolete machinery. Each requires about three times as many operators, at considerably higher salaries, as their provincial counterparts. A type-setter in London, using yesteryear's technology, earns considerably more than a professor of computer science for a job which a moderately trained teenager could do with ease on modern equipment. The London papers are not profitable and are subsidized by entrepreneurs who have made their fortunes in other fields. There have been serious attempts to modernize the papers and several strikes to obstruct the process. *The Times* was closed for many months on one occasion over such a dispute. The owner of Mirror Group newspapers, Robert Maxwell, threatened that the Group would have to close if serious over-manning is not removed and replaced by the introduction of IT. It has taken the threat of an imminent new national newspaper to be produced 80 per cent cheaper to obtain this reaction (whether Robert Maxwell will be able to put the change into effect remains to be seen). Information technology promotes competitiveness in terms of cost reductions with large-volume outputs (economies of scale). But the savings can be wider. As the *Nottingham Evening Post* illustrates, it may also become worthwhile to produce different products on the same equipment (economies of scope), because of the flexibility that IT affords. Such economies of scope and scale may also be available to manufacturing industry in general. In addition, IT may also help competitiveness by reducing lead and delivery times, reducing the carrying costs of stocks (through being able to cope with less stock) and by increasing quality and reducing scrap and waste (reductions in inspection costs may also accompany these types of savings).

On a wider front, the introduction of IT has implications for the success of whole sectors of industry. Very few companies, if any, are so arranged that they are independent of outside suppliers or sell all their produce within the company. They, therefore, depend to some extent both upon their suppliers' ability to provide goods efficiently and cheaply and upon the continued purchase of their goods by customers who are themselves manufacturing companies and who eventually sell to the end-user. A kind of 'food-chain' arrangement may be said to exist ranging from raw material suppliers at one end to end-users at the other. Suppliers of goods to other companies further along the chain are vulnerable if any of the organizations between them and the end-user becomes so inefficient that the market is lost. The loss of markets, particularly by companies towards the final-user end of the chain, is most likely to have a domino effect on their supplier firms. Such has been the experience in the United Kingdom, at least, for a number of years.

The benefit of IT in helping bring lower cost products to market derives not just from the actual machine operations that produce the goods but also from the influence of better *co-ordination* of the activities or their integration. Integration is something much talked about, little specified, little understood and even less achieved. If a company is represented as a three-dimensional set of activities, with senior management down to shop-floor employees as one axis, each function as another axis and each product or division as the third axis, then it is clear that integration involves vertical, horizontal and perhaps diagonal co-ordination of activities. It is a mistake to restrict integration to one of the dimensions only and a great deal of the attention that has been paid to the introduction of IT has tended to follow a unidimensional approach. Indeed, there are often formidable problems to be overcome in achieving even this degree of integration. But, although those who do achieve it are to be commended, there are also dangers inherent in this method. As an extreme, but illustrative example, IT might be introduced in the production of product X, enabling sales, the various departments in the stages of production and accounts to communicate with each other so that X is produced on time for customers and the sales revenue is also collected on time. However, this set of activities could be incompatible with the more strategic objectives of the business. For example, despite this achievement the firm could still be bankrupt. The integrational use of IT may quite conceivably depress the firm's performance rather than improving it.

The how of IT

Actually realizing the potential benefits of IT described in the previous section is not easy. In many cases where IT has been introduced, reliance has been placed upon a computer package to which the organization has subsequently had to adapt. But, adaptation is often not practical and the IT is then badly used or abandoned. Where specially designed computer programs have been introduced their degree of success may be marred by inadequate assessment of why IT is being introduced. What should be clear, therefore, is that the form of IT adopted should be appropriate to the circumstances facing a particular organization.

Thus, in deciding on how to manage the introduction of IT (which includes the decision not to do so) an organization needs to be able to assess its circumstances in a structured and coherent manner. Such an approach requires asking questions about the organization's relationship with its environment and about the organization's internal structure and workings. For both of these aspcts, *change* is an important element in the assessment procedure. Consideration of change involves not only the manner and speed of change of the external environment, but how the organization usually deals with change. It needs to be asked whether the normal means of dealing with change are appropriate for the change involved in the introduction of IT. An important element in coping with change is the nature of resistance to change and how that resistance is handled. Explicit analysis of the implications of change may enable it to be seen as presenting *opportunities* to achieve objectives rather than simply as a *threat*.

Dealing with the issues

To deal with the issues surrounding management of IT, we begin with a general treatment of the problems of dealing with change and develop the discussion into practical guidelines for those companies facing the introduction of IT.

Contrary to some popular belief, change produced by IT is not the first that has occurred in industry, nor is it the unique occasion on which change has been rapid. Chapter 2 sets out the nature of change, what is known about the way in which companies handle it, and why resistance to change might occur. Attention to these issues can enable managers of organizations to see change as offering not a threat but many opportunities. This discussion, therefore, addresses the way in which firms deal with the change involved with the introduction of IT, and these are taken up in detail in Chapter 3. In particular, Chapter 3 sets out a general framework for the management of the introduction of IT, including dealing with resistance to change. Within this framework the integration of activities afforded by IT is viewed on a multi-dimensional basis and it is shown that a firm has a choice of ways in which it can deal with IT. The need is to adopt an approach suitable for the particular firm in question. Chapter 4 develops the preceding two chapters to provide a practical procedure which allows the management of a firm to identify the appropriate route to the introduction of IT, and a methodology for carrying it out. The remaining chapters of the book, apart from the last one, provide detailed case study material which shows how the methodology developed earlier might be used in practice. The first case study chapter (Chapter 5) illustrates misguided shortcuts and failures and shows how the methodology can help identify problem areas. The second case study chapter (Chapter 6) deals with the more detailed aspects of systems analysis and design and demonstrates a more successful application where major problems of integration are involved. The final case study chapter deals with a different type of organization than the other case material. The introduction of IT in a hospital in the British National Health Service illustrates the issues and problems involved where the pressure to change is not from a rapidly changing competitive environment, in an organization whose management styles emphasize a different aspect of integration than that found in commercial firms. In the British National Health Service, line management authority is not a strong feature of the organizational structure, although there have recently been proposals to strengthen it. The main thrust of management style is consensus management which focuses on agreement between the nursing, medical and administrative professions at each level in the organization, on what is to be done. Horizontal integration is thus emphasized at the expense of vertical co-ordination. In making the comparison between these types of organizational style the importance of a multi-dimensional approach to integration is highlighted. The circumstances of the introduction of IT, namely well-publicized concern about the nature of patient care, also illustrate the opportunity provided by environmental factors in provoking change.

In all the case material a common unifying thread is clear. Since effecting the changes involved in introducing IT is often complex, in terms both of the technology itself and of the managerial issues, a need for an agent of change is apparent. This catalyst may come from either inside or outside the company, but in either case must have the *authority* to effect change and have the *support* of those for whom the change is intended.

The final chapter is rather more speculative in nature than the rest of the book, as it attempts to identify future trends in the introduction of IT. Emphasis is both on the side of the technology itself and on the management issues involved.

Reading this book

This book aims to assist all those who are interested in the introduction of IT into an organization. As such, there are parts of the book which are more likely to appeal to some readers rather than others. Those involved in the introduction of IT in their own companies are likely to find Chapters 4 to 7 of most practical relevance.

For those concerned with the more general issues of how organizations deal with change and with that concerning IT in particular, Chapters 2, 3 and 8 are recommended starting points. The book has, however, been written as an integrated whole (given that integration is a major theme in the book, it would be rather cowardly of us if it were not). It is hoped that readers approaching the subject from differing perspectives will gain something positive from the bringing together of the general and practical aspects involved in managing the introduction of IT.

References

C. A. Voss, 'The Management of New Manufacturing Technology,' *INRIA Conference on Production Systems*, Paris, April 23–6, 1985.

2 Change and IT

Introduction

Change is nothing new. The development of a modern industrialized society, by its very nature, involves a great deal of change over a prolonged period of time. The change resulting from the introduction of IT is usually regarded as being particularly rapid, although as we shall see, this may not necessarily be the case. This chapter will show that the need for and manner of adaptation to IT can be dealt with by drawing upon what is well known about how organizations and individuals deal with change in general.

Sources of change

Change concerns alterations to the manner in which actions are carried out. Actions may be broadly defined to include not only the carrying out of work tasks but also the supplying of goods to the market, the taking of management decisions, the organizational framework within which the decisions are taken and the values or ideologies which influence other actions.

The sources of change may be viewed as emanating from both outside and inside an organization. Outside factors can further be divided into those which are supply- or demand-related. Supply-related sources of change may for simplicity be regarded as deriving from the entry into the market-place of new techniques for carrying out tasks, and the techniques may refer either to more technologically advanced machines or to new management techniques.

Whether or not these techniques are taken up by a particular organization depends very much on demand factors.
Demand arises where the new technique supplied is
perceived to provide the solution to a problem faced by the
organization, adoption depending upon the price being
'right'. The nature of the problem may basically be twofold.
Firstly, adoption of a new technique may be an important
influence on a firm's ability to compete in the market-place,
particularly if competitors are also innovating. Where
competitors are not adopters the adopting organization may
improve its relative position in the market-place. Internal
factors may provide the second source of problems for
which the technique offers a solution. For example,
management may view the new technique as providing
better information for the control of a process, which could
not be achieved with an existing manual system.

The internal organizational effects of the changes
brought about by the introduction of IT (summarized in
Table 2.1) are threefold: the reduction/elimination of
clerical effort, more timely information, and the provision of

Table 2.1 The effects of IT in summary

Effect on organization	Benefits	Problems
1. Clerical effort eliminated/reduced	• Eliminates tedium • Redeployment to other tasks	• Could worsen industrial relations • Redundancies
2. More timely information	• Flexibility • Opportunities perceived earlier • Could eliminate or assist 'fire-fighting'	• Pressure on managers to manage • Laziness through over-reliance on machine
3. New opportunities	• New (integrated, unified) systems • Greater efficiency • More competitive business • Cost reduction • Less idiosyncratic judgement	• Revisions to familiar practice • Confusion • Managers not trained to cope/understand • Nature of management tasks may change

new opportunities for practice. In each of these areas, the introduction of IT brings the threat of problems as well as the opportunity for benefits to be derived.

The novel features of IT, its vastly increased range of applicability compared with older generation of computers arising from its cheapness, reliability, speed, accuracy, etc., and the present-day general increase in competitive and cost pressures coming at a time when the balance of power industrially has shifted back towards the employers, have served to bring a general pressure for its introduction in all types of organization. But to be clearer about the appropriateness and the effects of change on organizations, and of the change brought about by IT in particular, it is necessary to examine more closely how different organizations and individuals react to and deal with change. For there is no one 'right' answer which is applicable to all circumstances and all organizations and individuals. This point is as much appropriate to IT as it is to any other form of change.

Resistance to change

Whilst change may provide benefits to an organization, it is resistance if not outright disruption that attracts a great deal of attention when change is proposed. Such resistance may occur at various stages in the introduction of change and relate to a number of factors.

Figure 2.1 highlights the stages in the introduction of change where resistance may arise. For ease of exposition the implementation part of the process is considerably simplified from the more detailed treatment presented in subsequent chapters. Table 2.2 summarizes the sources of resistance from the main work groups in an organization. Taking the two figures together enables us to say something about the kind of resistance to be expected at each stage.

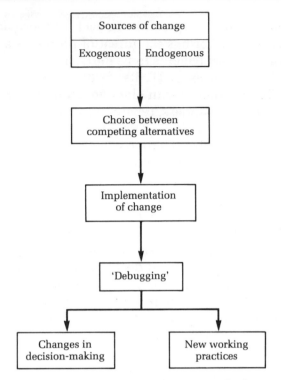

Figure 2.1 Stages in the introduction of change where resistance may be felt

The sources of change are treated as arising from outside the company (exogenous) or inside it (endogenous). In both cases change is seen to present itself initially as a choice between a number of competing alternatives. Where the organization has a protected market position such that few competitors exist, management may opt for a quiet life and resistance to outside change will take a rather passive form. Such a position may persist, however, only as long as competitors are prevented from entering the market-place. Management may also be able to resist pressure for internal change by opting for the quiet life, particularly where slack resources exist to absorb the results of not doing anything and where other work groups too resist change.

Table 2.2 Sources of resistance to change and work
groups in the organization

Work group	Sources of resistance
Management	• Change in superior–subordinate relationships • Loss of control over information • Threat to status and ego • Desire for quiet life • Incompetence
Employees as individuals	• Deskilling of task • Need to learn new skills • Change in superior–subordinate relationships • Threat of job loss • Rumour versus information • Increased job complexity
Informal work groups	• Resistance to ending/changing long-established inter-personal relationship • By-passing of new information systems
Trade unions	• Changing of 'craft' traditions • Loss of control over members • Changing job boundaries • Effects on bargaining position • Changing role of workplace officials

Management may do nothing because it is incompetent
or afraid of the unknown, though incompetence may
involve taking some action but of making an incorrect
choice! Even competent managers may choose between
competing alternatives in a way that is detrimental to the
aims of the company, but which has benefits for themselves. For example, choices may be made which minimize
the threat to the manager's status and ego or which at least
affect his loss of control over information. Of course, it may
not always be management prerogative to make the choice
between competing alternatives. A more participative style
of management may give employees a greater say in how
change is dealt with. Where employees are conservative

change may be resisted. Aside from participative management styles the strength of informal work groups or trade
unions in the workplace may constrain the choice that
management make as they know that the bargaining processes in the organization will only permit agreement to be
made upon a certain course of action.

The choice of alternatives is likely to influence the degree
of resistance to be experienced at the implementation stage,
as is the manner in which change is presented and dealt
with. Resistance here may relate either to proposed changes
in the way the task is *managed* and/or to proposed changes
in the task *itself*. Good superior–subordinate relationships
are not formed quickly, rather it takes a great deal of time for
mutual trust and understanding to be developed. The
attempt to implement change from 'on high' poses a threat
to such relationships. This is not to say that the superior–
subordinate relationships are immutable. On the contrary,
such relationships are likely to change constantly as
personnel change. However, the manner in which change is
dealt with is important. As the case material presented in
later chapters shows, a collaborative approach has a
number of advantages. Collaboration can help reduce if not
avoid resistance by defusing fear of the new. Involvement of
all employees in the process of change also brings the
benefit that the change introduced better fits the problem to
be solved. It is not only the organization which is trans-
formed through the process of innovation but also the
innovation itself. Employees who carry out the task have
intimate knowledge about that task which others are
unlikely to possess. Failure to take this knowledge into
account may result either in the solution not fitting the
problem or induce resistance so that those carrying out the
task by-pass the new technique wherever possible. By-
passing is particularly likely to occur in informal work
groups where interrelationships are particularly resistant to
change. Changes in the task itself may produce resistance
because of the threat or reality of deskilling of the task or,

indeed, its abolition. On the other hand, resistance may stem from the need to learn new skills or the need to cope with increased job complexity. Deskilling involves not only the redundancy of skills learnt over a period of time but also loss of status and the threat of loss of pay differentials that goes with it. On the other hand, as a study by Wilkinson has shown, it may be possible given the type of work and the attitude of managers and employees for new techniques to be used to *enhance* rather than *replace* existing skills.

Resistance from trade unions may arise in a number of areas. The most obvious is concern with the loss of members' jobs. However, behind this basic issue lie several others. Change in tasks may involve a move away from the 'craft' tradition of a trade union and bring it into conflict with other trade unions in the workplace, where they exist. The change in job boundaries which takes place means that a particular union may be striving to protect its members against job loss in direct competition with the members of another union. Trade unions may also experience loss of control over their members and a decline in their bargaining positions within the organization. Loss of control may arise where members perceive the changes as necessary to maintain the viability of the organization and preserve their jobs. A decline in a union's bargaining position may arise from management appeals over the heads of the union direct to the work-force and which are perceived as necessary where union recalcitrance severely disrupts the speed at which innovations need to be made for survival to be achieved. The workplace union officials may not fully appreciate the changed role they need to play. Where rapid change is inevitable the appropriate stance of the trade union may lie not simply in the resistance to job losses or erosion of differentials or resistance to the change *per se*, but rather in an approach that accepts the change but seeks full involvement in the way in which such change comes about.

It is unusual for any change to work acceptably at the first attempt so that an element of refinement, 'debugging', is required. The extent of necessary debugging depends greatly upon the innovation itself and the manner in which it has been introduced. It is at this stage that new working practices and changes in decision-making processes will crystallize. The establishment of new working practices may involve hardening of resistance, presenting management with a dilemma. Either the change is aborted, which at such a late stage may well be undesirable, or a trade-off is accepted where the innovation is able to function but at less than the desired level.

Given the importance of the way in which change is introduced into the organization in provoking resistance, it is important now to examine in detail how change may be dealt with.

Dealing with change

Change does not occur in isolation. As shown, the effects of change depend closely upon the nature of change itself and the characteristics of the individual and the organization.

Consider first the individual in a company and change, as portrayed in Figure 2.2. In deciding how to cope with a proposed change in the work task the individual's first reference point is how he deals with change in general. This response is seen to be influenced by personal goals and individual learning processes and by the management/ company and work group attitudes as far as inter-personal contacts are concerned. All these influences then colour the individual's approach to the changed task which is manifested in performance at the new task. Feedback on how previous changes that have been successfully coped with provides another important input into the individual's behaviour. Generally favourable prior experiences may help build up confidence to welcome and accept change,

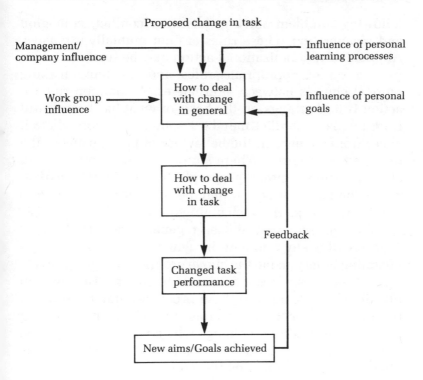

Figure 2.2 The individual and change

whereas past failure may reinforce resistance. Scope for conflict between the desired change and the individual may arise for a variety of reasons. For example, the proposed change may not meet the individual's personal goals of monetary rewards from doing a task or of job satisfaction. Alternatively, the individual's goals and learning processes may fit with a proposed change but be constrained by work group resistance.

The manner in which change is dealt with across the organization as a whole is not, however, the sum of each individual member's approach. If it were, the likely result would be chaos. Instead, change comes to be accommodated in terms of the basic ground rules for organizational action. Six principal ground rules may be observed: rule following, problem solving, learning, conflict, contagion and regeneration. These rules are not mutually exclusive. Alternatively, organizational action may be seen as derived from a set of appropriate rules and involving making rational choices between alternatives. A common rule for action is to do things on the basis of what has been learnt from the past. Conflict may be a source of action where it arises from changes in the behaviour of participants or the reasons they control. Where similar organizations exist in close proximity, either geographically or in the market-place, the basis for action may be transferred from one to the other. The fact that a changing mix of participants exists in an organization may of itself regenerate action.

Where the environment in which an organization is operating is very stable the above ground rules may provide stable processes of responsiveness to change. However, in practice the outcomes of these processes may be different from expected or the environment itself may be changing rapidly. Complexities in change which produce unexpected outcomes may arise for a number of reasons. First the organization may mis-time the process of change so that it either lags behind or goes in advance of what is compatible with the environment. Second, the organization may mis-interpret the causal link between change required inter-nally and change in the environment. Third, change is unlikely to be an isolated event but rather involves a number of parallel factors. Such concurrence of change may produce undesirable joint outcomes. To these points may be added others which concern the nature of the organization itself. Organizations face many problems but are only able to identify a limited number of solutions. Change may, therefore, centre around matching a solution to a problem rather than the other way round. As such solutions are unlikely to be specific to the particular organization, change may involve both transformation of the innovation itself and of the organization. This process may well extend to development and redefinition of the goals of the organization as previously unthought-of possibilities arise. To the extent that organizations create their own environments through their behaviour, changes in behaviour influence changes in the environment. Such interactions clearly imply that the process of change may not only produce unsuspected and indeterminate outcomes, but also that the process is likely to be dynamic and continuous. An important prerequisite, therefore, for a successful organization is that it recognizes, accepts and deals with continuous change. Such changes may, however, take place at different rates at different points in time.

Rapid, violent, or unexpected change, as implied by the introduction of IT, may have a profound impact upon both the shape of the organization and the way in which it behaves. All organizations do not react in the same way to such change, as may be seen from Table 2.3. Reactions may be classified in terms of taking advantage of an opportunity, ignoring the change, weathering the storm (Resistance) or disruption, following a study of the effects of a doctors' strike on hospitals in California (see Meyer, 1982). Although this study focused on the effects of a one-off short-lived environmental jolt, general lessons may be drawn from it which may be applicable to the rapid change implied by the introduction of IT. Four principal influences on the type of reaction may be identified: the type of strategy planned by an organization prior to the change; the ideology of the organization; the organizational management structure and the degree and type of slack resources which exist. Of these four influences, strategy and ideology provide the best indicators of how an organization will adapt to rapid change, according to Meyer. Organizations which see rapid change as presenting new opportunities are characteristically dynamic: they have loosely linked organizational structures, ideology shifting with changes in power, and the frequent scanning of and movement into and out of numerous market environments. Organizations that can be described as ignoring change perceive

Table 2.3 Influences on reactions to rapid change

Influence	Opportunity	Ignore	'Weather the storm' (resist)	Disruption
Strategy	• Frequent scanning of numerous environments • Volatile market niches	• Broad range of product areas • Exploit new opportunities and keep old ones	• Defender of market niches • Narrow focus of markets	• Narrow, specialised market • Conventional marketing policy • Unwillingness to adjust strategy
Ideology	• High entre-preneurial • Pluralistic values • Power shifts in response to issues	• Corporate approach • Cybernetic control • Divisions own ideologies	• Emphasis on efficiency, predictability, self-reliance • Insulate organization from environ-ment	• Lack of employee loyalty • Discordant ideology
Structure	• Loosely coupled structure based on products	• Divisionalized semi-autonomous	• Functional and fully integrated • Little cross-department collaboration as few problems	• Emphasises divisions between work-force and management
Slack resources	• Small financial reserves • Over-staffing • Large amount of technology • Tight control	• Moderate reserves • Moderate staffing • Moderate amount of technology • Large capital reserves	• Large financial reserves • Understaffing • Low amount of technology • Low amount of capital	• Generally less slack available

Source: Adapted from Meyer, A., 'Adapting to Environmental Jolts', *Administrative Science Quarterly*, Vol. 27, No. 4, 1982.

adaptation as an automatic ability to adjust given by presence in a diversified range of products under a semi-autonomous divisionalized management structure. In contrast to these types of reactions, organizations which seek to 'weather the storm' or which suffer disruption try to close themselves off from environmental factors and seek to preserve entrenched specialized positions. The differences relate closely to the extent of slack resources available, the extent to which decisions within the organization are amplified and the consequent level of employee loyalty and divergence of management ideology from that of the organization as a whole.

These influences on the reaction to rapid change suggest how the organization deals with the mechanics of change, or what might be termed organizational learning. As might be expected, different organizations learn in different ways. Table 2.4 illustrates one approach characterizing the various ways in which organizations adapt. Learning systems may be categorized along two axes: one expressing individual to organizational orientation and the other orientation ranging from evolution to formal design. In any organization, adaptation will relate to individual members as well as to the organization itself and will consist of

Table 2.4 Typology of organizational learning systems

		Individual—organisational dimension		
		More individual oriented ◄————►		More organisationally oriented
Evolutionary design dimension	More evolutionary ▲ ⎪ ⎪ ▼ More designed	One-man institution	Mythological learning system	Information-seeking culture
		Participative learning system	Formal management system	Bureaucratic learning system

Source: P. Shrivastava, 'A Typology of Organisational Learning Systems', *J. Management Studies* Vol. 20, 1983.

evolutionary as well as designed or implanted elements. For example, an individual's behaviour evolves over time according to experience, whilst the organization as a whole may be characterized by a formally designed bureaucratic structure in which learning follows set prescribed rules. Since these organizational learning systems are not mutually exclusive, it follows that for the organization to be able to adapt efficiently, care should be taken to ensure that these systems are not in conflict. The failure of many of the earlier cybernetics-based management information systems in companies is widely attributed to the failure of the designers to take account of what was already happening in the organization. In this case, for example, the views of individuals were ignored, little participation in changing the system was involved, with the consequent result that informal groups were reinforced so as to by-pass the formal system and to produce the kind of resistance to change already discussed.

The need to avoid conflict in learning systems does not, however, imply the appropriateness of a particular con-figuration of systems. As the influences on the reactions to change and the causes of resistance imply, organizations may be considered to possess the ability to exercise choice. But choice does not take place in a vacuum, it is influenced by factors both external and internal to the organization. External factors include the state of the market environment in which the organization is operating, whether it is stable or dynamic, whether it is heterogeneous or homogenous (i.e. many or one market), and whether the organization possess a greater or lesser degree of control over its environment (e.g. competitive power). Internal to the organization, the importance of behavioural factors, such as the motivation of employees, management styles, political processes and informal groups, need to be taken into account as well as the organization's technology, its ownership form (subsidiary or parent, family held or publicly-quoted), its size, its age and its position in the life-cycle. These factors also contribute to the organizational learning systems which exist at a particular point in time and which may themselves circumscribe the changes that are feasible.

Conclusions

The ways in which the above factors are influential in effecting the change necessitated by the introduction of IT are discussed in the following chapter. The general implications, however, for the management of the introduction of IT are that IT *by itself* does not affect the nature of the task nor the organization. Rather it is particular features of the organization itself and the environment in which it operates which are the crucial factors. It is, therefore, appreciation of these rather than the capabilities of particular types of hardware or software which is the starting-point in the introduction of IT into the organization.

References

J. G. March, 'Footnotes to Organizational Change', *Administrative Science Quarterly*, Vol. 26, No. 4, 1981.

A. D. Meyer, 'Adapting to Environmental Jolts', *Administrative Science Quarterly*, Vol. 27, No. 4, 1982.

R. G. Murdick, *MIS Concepts and Design*, Prentice-Hall, 1980.

P. Shrivastava, 'A Typology of Organisational Learning Systems', *J. Management Studies*, Vol. 20, No. 1, 1983.

3 Managing the introduction of IT: the management perspective

Introduction

Early management experience with the introduction of computers and more recently with IT, has emphasized categories such as office automation, or CAD/CAM. Where computers and IT have been introduced, the main involvement has usually come from specialist electronic data processing (EDP) staff rather than from line management. In many companies, though, IT is simply absent. Specialist EDP staff are likely to be highly familiar with the technical capabilities of hardware and software having the benefits of a number of years of training and experience. Managers cannot and should not be expected to be familiar with IT to such a level of detail. But what they should be in a position to know is how the capabilities of IT can be fully and realistically applied to their particular organization. To achieve that level of knowledge requires a positive learning process on the manager's part. Without this managers are vulnerable to computer systems sales people or to over-enthusiastic members of their own organization. Managers need to be in a position to decide for themselves on a rational basis whether salesmen's claims represent exaggerations or opportunities. This chapter discusses the main issues in the management of the introduction of IT and draws attention to the implications for each level in the organization, the effects on the organizational structure, the requirements for management styles and the effects on work-force motivation.

Corporate strategy, competitiveness and IT

Most applications of IT have been on the operational level of the organization. However, as may be seen from Figure 3.1, three levels of organizational control and decision-making may be highlighted: strategic, tactical and operational. For any organization to function effectively and efficiently, the behaviour of each level should be consistent with that of the other two. Should this not be the case, then, for example, the operational level may engage in action which does not enable corporate strategic objectives to be met. As IT becomes more accessible to a wider range of people within an organization, and the reduction in cost enables individual managers to take the initiative in acquiring particular items of IT, the likelihood is that without an overall co-ordination of IT, its use is likely to become increasingly fragmented. The sum of the individual

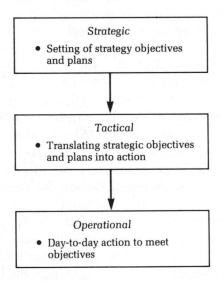

Figure 3.1 Control and decision-making levels in the organization

initiatives in each department may not, therefore, be the best possible for the firm as a whole.

Before the purchase of any item of IT, the ideal is to assess the opportunities presented by IT at each level in the organization, and to adopt a policy which allows the introduction of IT in a consistent manner throughout the company. This is perhaps much easier said than done, but if a serious attempt is to be made to use IT it is an indispensable exercise. It may be better to give up altogether the idea of using IT, rather than go about it in a hit-or-miss way.

Some of the major opportunities presented by IT are summarized in Figure 3.2, where a distinction is made between strategic and tactical/operational opportunities. Each is now addressed in detail.

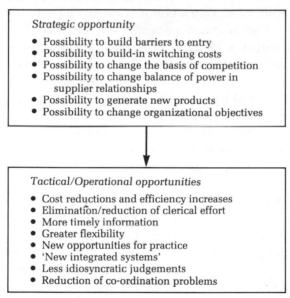

Figure 3.2 Broad opportunities presented by IT

Strategic

At this level IT can contribute both to the attainment of given corporate objectives and to the development and realization of new objectives. The attainment of corporate objectives requires that an organization successfully deals with the competitive environment in which it operates. According to Porter a competitive environment has five key elements: other competitors in the same industry, customers, suppliers, potential entrants to the industry, and substitute products and services. Figure 3.2, shows that IT may provide strategic opportunities for dealing with these elements. Of course, it is important to bear in mind that IT is not necessarily the only way of exploiting these opportunities!

First, by adopting IT early or in such a way that competitors cannot replicate it, an organization may be able to raise a barrier to other organizations entering the market. For example, to service a client company's particular needs a sophisticated software package may be developed which contains features leading to further development. It may then be difficult for a potential competitor to develop an alternative package which is sufficiently more advanced or cheaper to tempt the client to switch. Such barriers to entry may, however, be removed over time as IT undergoes rapid changes and new opportunities are perceived. The initially well-placed organization may then be faced with a barrier-to-exit problem as it has invested heavily in IT expertise and systems which are rapidly becoming obsolete.

Barriers to exit may be reinforced by a client becoming dependent upon the supplier's product, such that the costs of switching to another supplier, with possibly another system, are prohibitive and are raised by the need to come to terms with a new system and establish new working relationships. For example, DPCE (Data Processing Custom Engineering, plc) has grown rapidly as a provider of computer-systems maintenance services. The company usually locates engineers quasi-permanently on the customer's site, as the client's systems are large and complex, and service contracts cover all the makes of IT that the customer has in use. There are clear switching costs benefits to the supplier, and benefits to the customer from the need to deal with only one maintenance contractor.

However, the possibility also arises that the balance of power in customer-supplier relationships might be changed. In the previous example, the possibility clearly exists for the supplier to exploit its position to earn monopoly profits. Client companies, therefore, need to keep the extent of increased dependence on a supplier under review. Another facet of the change in customer-supplier relationships stems from the use of Just-in-Time (JIT) delivery systems. These systems have been particularly used in the automobile industry and enable stock levels to be substantially reduced with resultant cost savings. These delivery systems rely for their success on close liaison between customers and suppliers. As the level of inventory is reduced, the customer has few buffer stocks available to meet breakdowns in supply. The potential exists, therefore, for suppliers to exploit the dependence of customers on regular on-time suppliers. Customers have been able to reduce this threat by setting-up multiple-sourcing systems so that no single supplier can dictate terms.

Competitive strategies of firms may be considered to be conducted on one of three main principles. First, a company may seek to produce at lower cost than its competitors. Second, a company may offer a different mix of products (including quality differences). Third, a company may seek to specialize in a particular niche in the market. All three involve the firm performing at least as effectively and efficiently as competitors. Information technology can provide the opportunity to produce at lower cost, through, for example, the use of numerically controlled machine tools to increase machine efficiency, reductions in design costs, or staffing reductions. But for some products it can also enable the basis of competition to be changed, mainly from lower cost to product differentation or vice versa. In the former case, to take the example of the financial services industry, IT is becoming important in enabling the providers of financial services to offer a wider area of services in areas beyond those with which they are normally associated. In this way the demands of increasingly sophisticated customers can be met, coupled with increased convenience. Movements away from product differentation to lower cost competition may occur where the potential reductions in cost from IT-assisted methods of production substantially outweigh the benefits to customers from having tailor-made products.

The extent of product differentation may also be extended through IT so that entirely new products are offered to the market, for example, by the application of IT to a technique for analysis, so that a customer may use the tool himself rather than having to use the services of a specialist agency.

All the preceding opportunities offered by IT make change in strategic corporate objectives possible. Such changes may be seen in terms of an upward revision in the percentage return on investment earned, market shares held, and the scope of particular markets in which the organization wishes to operate successfully. On a more ideological level, the opportunities provided by IT, both at the strategic level and the way these feed down to the tactical and operational levels, may lead to a reassessment of objectives namely, of what the organization is for. Some would argue that consideration of IT opportunities provides the possibility for a radical review of the company's objectives (which may involve formulating them clearly for the first time), and organization structure so as to emphasize a more democratic approach to management, improvements in the quality of the work task and less emphasis on the profit motive. This particular issue is discussed in more detail below under management styles and motivation. A movement in this direction is one option in dealing with change (see Chapter 2). There is, however, an inescapable need to set strategic objectives clearly and realistically in the light of the competitive environment in which the organization operates. Schematically, the determination of an IT strategy may be shown as in Figure 3.3. Internal factors also influence strategic objectives, which determine IT strategy. The IT strategy adopted has impacts at the lower organizational levels, in terms of the opportunities detailed in Figure 3.2, and on the way IT is perceived and

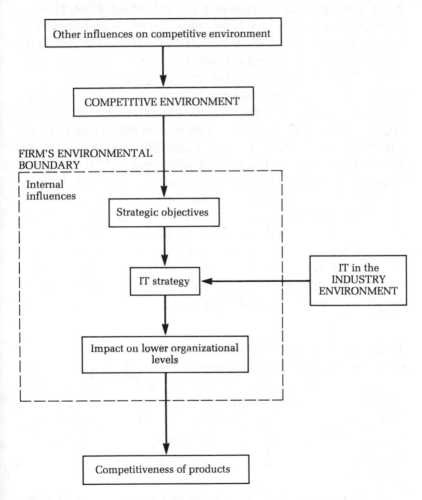

Figure 3.3 Determining IT strategy

adopted in the industry in which the organization operates, in general. This in turn affects the future competitive environment as do the results of the IT strategy at the lower organization levels, insofar as the competitiveness of products is changed.

The relationship between the competitive environment and the detailed IT strategy is further developed in Table 3.1. Four principal IT strategies are identified. First, IT may be seen to pervade the whole organization, with benefits at the operational level, in co-ordinating activities at different levels and at the strategic level, but also requiring a great deal of senior level monitoring and planning to make necessary changes. This may be particularly true of fast-growing, highly competitive industries where existing and new IT applications are necessary to maintain or attain competitive advantages. Secondly, IT may currently not be important but developments in the market-place and in IT techniques indicate that it will become important in the near future. A third IT strategy focuses attention on its use for day-to-day operations and may be particularly important in stable or declining markets where low-cost, efficient delivery etc., are essential aspects of competitiveness. The relatively unchanging nature of the environment lessens the importance of the strategic element of IT. The fourth IT strategy is supportive, and essentially this means that IT is not crucial

Table 3.1 Types of IT strategy

| Type of IT strategy | Competitive environment | | |
	Fast-growing, highly competitive	Stable	Declining
Pervasive	H	L	H/L
Potential	H	L	H/L
Day-to-day	L	H	H/L
Supportive	L	H	H/L

H = Strategy highly appropriate; L = Strategy less appropriate to success at any level in the organization. The appropriate IT strategy in a declining industry is somewhat more indeterminate, depending upon the speed and variability of decline and the extent of the competition. The influences on the competitive environment of IT and other factors, such as competitors, customers, suppliers, new entrants or substitutes, mean that the type of IT strategy adopted must be reviewed to take account of changed circumstances.

Tactical/operational

The strategic opportunities presented by IT have mainly related to the way in which the organization interfaces with its competitive environment. These factors feed through into the organization itself in the way objectives are affected and the resultant implications for the lower levels of the organization. Figure 3.2 indicates some of the broad opportunities that IT may present at these tactical and operational levels. These opportunities, though, may also hide very serious management implications.

Greater flexibility in production scheduling may be possible through the IT's data handling capabilities, but the by-passing of decision-making by managers or production controllers may, however, remove useful flexibility. Reliance on complex algorithms alone rather than on the use of IT to enhance individual decisions may in fact reduce flexibility. Exclusive emphasis on the technology in achieving integrated systems to improve co-ordination, without awareness of the managerial issues can lead to failure. Of course, there are well-defined circumstances where sophisticated algorithms can provide the necessary benefits of IT. But these are really a special case of a general managerial problem. There is growing recent evidence that, contrary to expectations, firms are finding that the manufacturing systems they have acquired are not flexible at all and cannot cope with changed circumstances (see Voss, 1985).

It is therefore necessary to discuss the managerial issues in detail.

Organizational structure and control

General

The organizational structures to be found in firms derive from the fourteen principles of management first set down by Fayol. These principles may be listed as follows:

- Division of work; specialization of tasks.
- Authority and responsibility. Authority is the right to give orders and responsibility relates to ensuring they are carried out.
- Discipline; to ensure that behaviour is directed towards achieving objectives.
- Unity of command. Employees should only be the 'servant of one master' (organization of employees).
- Unity of direction. One head and one plan for a group of activities having the same objectives (organization of the firm).
- Interest of the organization should prevail over the interests of an individual or a group within the organization.
- Remuneration should be fair and afford satisfaction to both employees and the firm.
- Centralizing of authority, the desired level being dependent on circumstances.
- Scalar chain of command from the ultimate authority to the lowest rank.
- Order; 'a place for everyone and everyone in their place' within the organization.
- Equity and a sense of justice should pervade the organization in order to elicit loyalty from its members.
- Stability and tenure to enable employees to adapt to their work and to perform it effectively.

- Initiative should be encouraged amongst all employees of the organization to encourage satisfaction in carrying out tasks.
- *Esprit de corps* means an emphasis on teamwork, co-operation and interpersonal relationships. This recognizes the importance of communication in all aspects of management.

If we look at Figure 3.4 we can see a typical organization chart of a company that reflects many of the above principles. The scalar principle gives us the hierarchy of command from the Managing Director at the top to the Sales Managers and Production Managers at the bottom. Moreover, unity of direction is also observed both for the firm as a whole and for each directorate. If we work upwards, unity of command is evident as each occupier of a post only refers to one immediate superior.

As regards the division of work, this is seen in the breakdown of the firms into finance, marketing, production, management service and research functions, with sub-divisions of each for the various specialized tasks involved. Such departmentalization as this illustrates what is to be done in the firm. Departmentalization by function is only one way of dividing up the firm into manageable sub-units. We can also deparmentalize by numbers, territories, products, types of customers, etc. In some companies combinations of the above may be found, for example, where a matrix organization exists. This method combines functional and product forms of departmentalization. An example illustrates how this works, where a company is producing a number of products (or projects) a manager is put in charge of each, and has subordinates accordingly. But, although each product will require functional activities, such as sales, design, refinement, assembly, etc., it may not require them all the time. Particularly design functions are not constantly required. Matrix organization thus allows for flexibility in the utilization of

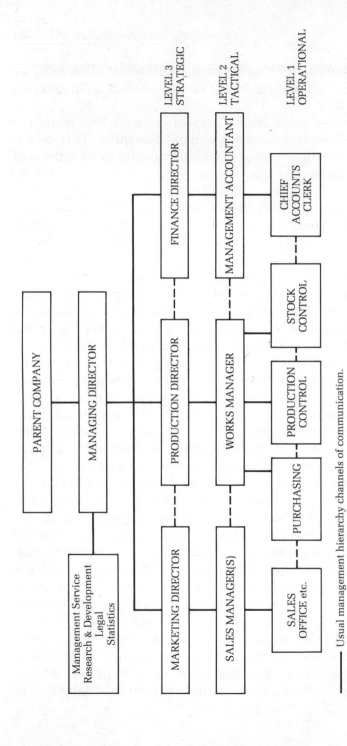

Figure 3.4 Typical organization chart showing control levels and communication links

PARENT COMPANY

MANAGING DIRECTOR

Management Service
Research & Development
Legal
Statistics

MARKETING DIRECTOR

PRODUCTION DIRECTOR

FINANCE DIRECTOR
— LEVEL 3
STRATEGIC

SALES MANAGER(S)

WORKS MANAGER

MANAGEMENT ACCOUNTANT
— LEVEL 2
TACTICAL

SALES OFFICE etc.

PURCHASING

PRODUCTION CONTROL

STOCK CONTROL

CHIEF ACCOUNTS CLERK
— LEVEL 1
OPERATIONAL

—— Usual management hierarchy channels of communication.

- - - Channels of cross communication between departments at the same level.

certain functions whilst maintaining the form of the organization.

In any form of organization a clear distinction needs to be drawn between departmentalization and line and staff relationships. Line and staff are distinguished by their authority relationships, not by what they do. The nature of line authority is apparent from the scalar principle, already mentioned. It is an authority relationship in which a superior exercises direct supervision over a subordinate. Hence the authority relationship is in a direct line. Staff functions tend to be advisory, in relation to the other functions of the firm. For example, the head of public relations may be regarded as advisory to the board. Hence, within departments, there may be both line and staff relationships and within the organization as a whole some departments may stand in a line or staff relationship to others.

Fayol's principles of authority and responsibility introduce notions of a 'span of control', that is the number of subordinates which a manager has authority over. The optimum number for a span of control will depend upon circumstances.

This type of approach tends to emphasize a rather rigid hierarchy of authority, what has been termed a 'mechanistic management structure, being characterized by rigidly defined tasks and central communication. Writers who have emphasized the human aspects of work refer to the benefits to be derived from allowing the full development of the individual, and favour a more fluid or 'organic' view of the management structure which features continual adjustment of tasks, and a network structure of control with vertical and horizontal communications.

Recent developments recognize the merits of each of these extreme forms of organization. But rather than asserting that one or the other is universally applicable, the appropriate form of organization is considered to depend on circumstances. Whether a rigid or flexible organization structure should be used depends on the environment in which the firm is operating, the size of the firm, whether the firm is independently owned or a subsidiary of a larger company, and the type of technology possessed.

When the environment, for example, the firm's market or the general economy, is relatively stable and unchanging, a rigid management hierarchy may be used, as tasks are unlikely to change rapidly. On the other hand, in unstable and changing environments a more flexible management is needed. The issue of size and the extent to which a formal management hierarchy exists, with different levels of management control (long-term, medium-term and short-term) is important in this book, as many of the firms to which it applies are at the smaller end of the spectrum. In larger firms these three control levels are likely to be clearly distinguishable independently of an organic or mechanistic organization structure. However, the smaller the firm the more it would be expected that the distinction between the levels becomes increasingly blurred.

Different ownership forms can have an important influence on the management organization. Long-term planning functions may be taken on by the parent company for a subsidiary and the co-ordination of sales and production activities in the subsidiary may be constrained by decisions taken by the parent. Such influences can be beneficial, if the management organization was weak or poorly maintained when the company was independent, but care is needed to ensure that any changes they bring about are accepted by the work-force and do not produce informal decision channels.

The type of technology with which the firm operates can also influence the form of organization. Unit and small batch producers tend towards personal and unitary types of managerial control, and large batch and mass producers are characterized by more mixed management control methods. In other words, the degree of flexibility inherent in the production technology influences the flexibility of the management hierarchy.

IT issues

The opportunities for improved control that IT provides, which have been outlined earlier, suggest certain implications for the organization structure. The ready transmission of information focuses attention on interdependencies between departments and tasks, calls into question traditional departmental and task boundaries, and affects barriers to the vertical transmission of information. A greater integration of activities therefore becomes feasible.

The major issue is whether integration will be achieved by increasing centralization of decision-making or by increased decentralization. Centralization is held to increase efficiency, whilst decentralization is held to provide increased flexibility and speed in decision-making, and greater motivation by lower level managers as they have greater responsibility.

IT may help increase centralization as comprehensive and current information can be passed direct from operational to senior management, by-passing middle management levels. These intermediate levels can, therefore, be removed or reduced producing a flattened management hierarchy. Such simplified structures may enable senior management to co-ordinate operational activities without the problem of wide spans of control. These arguments for centralization are reinforced by competitive and financial pressures which call for reductions in the higher levels of managerial overheads which matrix forms of management have contributed to.

Alternatively, decentralization may be preferred as IT enables all departments to be linked through a computer network and through the provision of 'better' information to lower levels enhances their ability to make informed decisions previously possible only for senior management.

There are problems in moving in either direction. Increasing centralization may not be warranted as flexibility of decision-making is required at lower levels to cope with changed circumstances. Increasing senior management involvement in the day-to-day running of the business may be dangerous if it distracts attention from consideration of strategic issues.

Increased decentralization may be hindered by delays and inadequacies in the development of tailor-made, integrated software as the case studies of Buchanan and Boddy have illustrated. There is also the danger in decentralization that lower level action will depart from the organization's overall strategy.

But what actually happens may not be a simple function of the new-found access to IT. The competitive environment and the behaviour of management are important influences. A survey by Robey suggests that any increase in centralization or decentralization will relate to the variety and variability of the competitive environment. As described above, in stable environments with homogeneous products, increased centralization is more appropriate, whilst in dynamic environments with multiple products decentralization is needed to deal with increased uncertainty and unpredictability; the size of the organization, the ownership form and the nature of the production technology will also influence the degree of centralization or decentralization. The case studies of Buchanan and Boddy draw attention to the significance of management behaviour in introducing new specialist groups, new management hierarchies and new positions to deal with IT. These kinds of developments may be detrimental to both centralized or decentralized structures as they can cut across interdependencies between functions, take operational control away from those closest to the task, and interfere with the vertical flow of information in the organization. As size and cost are reduced and IT becomes increasingly accessible to non-specialists the need for and size of specialist IT functions can be reassessed. As a result, for example, the EDP department in an organization may come to provide a central *servicing* function and specialist *assistance* rather than acting on line functions. Part of its specialist assistance role may be to develop training packages to enable line managers to take better advantage of opportunities.

The extent to which desirable adjustments are possible is a function of the organizational culture and its learning systems, as we have seen in Chapter 2. National cultures are also significant: similar organizations located in different countries will adapt differently. The study by Jacobs *et al*. of the way change is handled in West Germany and the United Kingdom vividly illustrates these differences. Cultural differences will affect such things as levels of resistance, changes in motivation, the behaviour and importance of informal groups and the political pressures in the firms which handle change.

Leadership and the introduction of IT

Early approaches to management of leadership took the view that managers could rely on formal organizational relations to get the work done. However, beginning with the work of Elton Mayo which highlighted the effects of participation in employee motivation, attention became focused upon different styles of management. Likert, for example, identified four systems of management style. System 1, exploitive-authoritative, is characterized by decision-making at the top of management hierarchy, downward communication flows and the use of orders and threats to obtain motivation towards organizational goals. The benevolent-authoritative approach of System 2, is still characterized by decision-making at the top, but allows for some delegation. Upward communication flows are limited to what the bosses want to hear. Rewards are used by management to encourage performance, as they also are in System 3, the consultative system. Here communication is more of a two-way process, up and down the hierarchy, and whilst some involvement of subordinates in decision-making is encouraged, most decisions are still made at the top. It is only in System 4, the participative system, where there is full group participation, and the flow of communications are down, up and across the organization. Widespread decision making occurs with greater involvement by members of the organization and a greater identification by them with the organization's goals. In addition, the relationships between manager and subordinate are seen as 'supportive', that is they build and maintain the sense of personal worth and importance of the individual. It is in System 4, argues Likert, that better performance is likely, because of greater involvement and hence greater fulfilment by subordinates.

McGregor adopts a similar approach characterizing managerial or leadership styles in terms of Theory X and Theory Y. Theory X typifies the traditional management view: humans dislike work and will avoid it if possible; they need coercion, control, direction and punishment if they are to achieve organizational goals; and humans want to be directed, to avoid responsibility, and have little ambition. Theory Y represents a more participative or democratic type of management. Work is seen as being as natural as play or rest. If individuals are committed to an objective they will exercise self-direction and self-control, and under proper conditions will learn to accept and seek responsibility. Hence, under Theory X the potential of the average person is not being fully used, and change to a Theory Y approach can cause many more of the individuals in the organization to contribute to problem solving. Argyris too argues for a more participative approach in management. If management provides the means for individuals to mature and be treated as mature individuals, they will not become frustrated and act inconsistently with organizational goals. A final example in the argument for a more participative approach comes from the studies by White and Lippitt on leadership styles in task-oriented groups. Democratically led groups were found to produce a higher quality of work and be able to function without the leader. In autocratically led groups output was higher and quality lower, the groups could not function alone, and when these groups were left to their own devices, performance, morale and satisfaction were all lower than in a democratically led group.

More recent research, however, has questioned the universal applicability of the distinction between authoritative and participative styles of management. As was indicated in the previous section, the appropriate management style may well be a function of the circumstances faced by the organization. What might be appropriate in one firm may not be for another. As we have seen in the previous section, the type of context is generally considered to have four main aspects—the environment in which the firm is operating, its technology, its size and the type of ownership. Each of these factors affects the type of problem that the leader has to deal with.

The appropriate solution may be modelled as a position relative to two areas, one representing the degree of necessary information available to the leader and the other the acceptability of the solution to subordinates on the other. Studies indicate that when a leader possesses all the information necessary to solve the problem and the solution is acceptable to subordinates, the appropriate leadership style omits participation. Alternatively, when information is dispersed and staff do not accept the decision, more participation is required. General participation, higher satisfaction, higher motivation and greater performance do not always, therefore, go together. Indeed, the expectancy theory of motivation suggests that an individual's motivation to carry out a task is a function of his perception that doing so will bring the desired reward. The means of maximizing an individual's expectancies comes from obtaining that blend of leadership styles, job, and payment structures which strengthens the link between effort, performance and rewards. The successful leadership style then is one that is responsive, that is, involves greater or lesser participation, according to the type of problem. This point has certain implications for the motivation of leaders or managers themselves. Writers on motivation such as Maslow, Herzberg and McClelland stress the importance of the satisfaction of needs. Successful managers are seen to desire a high level of satisfaction (Maslow's self-actualization) and are motivated by a sense of achievement and recognition, and relish responsibility and challenges. As has been noted by Davis, successful leaders must possess 'psychological maturity', which includes the traits of intelligence, social maturity, inner motivation and respect for human dignity. In other words, successful leaders need to possess a wide range of skills.

The implications of this discussion for managing the introduction of IT may be analysed as follows. As we have seen already, change, even that implied by IT, is not always necessarily rapid, as organizations operate in competitive environments which change at different rates. Depending upon circumstances, the role of IT in the organization will range from persuasive to supportive, and will be concerned with the attainment of strategic and tactical/operational objectives. These objectives, as has been seen, may seek to improve efficiency/performance or to improve managerial control *per se*. Evidence suggests that the introduction of IT is entrepreneurial in nature, in the sense that an individual or group within the organization perceives an opportunity where IT may help satisfy some objective. This 'promoter' is not necessarily in a senior management position in the company. The manner in which change is effected is a function of the information-acceptability trade-off outlined earlier. The amount of information available to the promoter relates not just to the rapidity of change, but to his level and influence in the organization and his skill both in terms of IT and generally. The acceptability of change to other members of the organization relates to political processes. Political processes will influence the manner in which conflicting objectives between 'promoters' and other organizational members are resolved. As we noted in Chapter 2, a very real danger exists that resistance to change will be encountered if the approach to it does not take proper account of the realities of the situation. Such resistance may take various forms, a principal one of which is an increase in the power of informal work groups in by-passing changed procedures and tasks. Depending on the information-acceptability trade-off, various methods are available to deal with resistance to change (see Table 3.2). According to the extent of resistance anticipated, the relative power of 'promoters' with respect to 'resistors', the dispersion of information holding and the consequences of resistance, one of six approaches may be used. Of particular interest are the approaches which involve some form of collaboration since these highlight the need for a 'promoter', who while initiating and promoting the introduction of change takes account of the needs and objectives of others in the organization. This has the added benefit in that in making use of the expertise of others, the form of change may be modified so that it properly fits the situation. There may be at the outset some uncertainty as to what the eventual outcome will be, but this should be outweighed by the high probability that it will be accepted and will work. Hence, for example, unanticipated changes in working procedures such as job rotation may make a considerable positive contribution to the successful implementation of change.

However, problems may arise from three main sources. The first is where the competitive environment indicates a different role for IT than that advocated by the promoter. The second is a lack of co-ordination between levels of the organization, especially where several promoters are attempting to introduce change. The third source of problems is attempts of promoters to override strategic and tactical/operational objectives and human factors in order to obtain what are perceived as improvements in automatic

Table 3.2 Dealing with resistance to change

Approach	Application	Benefits	Problems
Education	Where is lack of accurate information	Encourages employees to help implement change	Time-consuming
Participation	Where initiators do not possess all information and where others have power to resist	Helps commitment to change and change more likely to be appropriate	Time-consuming
Support	Where resistance stems from problems in adjustment	May be only method suitable where are adjustment problems	Time-consuming, expensive, risk of failure quite high
Negotiation	Where individual or group has something to lose and has power to resist	Where draws on established negotiating procedures may be relatively easy way of over-riding resistance	May trigger demands for negotiation from others
Manipulation	Where above will not work or are expensive	Can be quick and inexpensive	Stores up future problems if groups feel manipulated
Coercion	Where is need for speed and initiators possess power	Speedy and effective	Risky as may produce future resistance

Source: adapted from J. P. Kotter and L. A. Schlesinger, 'Choosing Strategies for Change', *Harvard Business Review*, March/April 1979.

control. Case studies undertaken by Buchanan and Boddy illustrate how this last source of problem may arise in the efforts of middle and lower managers to increase the predictability, consistency, orderliness and reliability of operations. Their study indicates that misplaced optimism about the application of IT and misunderstanding of the importance of the human factors may lead to problems. Solutions to these three types of problems may lie in the development of a co-ordinated IT strategy, which, however, must recognize the importance of someone to fill the role of promoter to ensure that change is carried through.

In some organizations the introduction of IT is impeded by a lack of skills or because the person who could fulfill the role of promoter cannot be diverted from his normal tasks or is unacceptable to other members of the organization. In these kinds of situations agents of change external to the organization, consultants, have a role to play. Whilst potentially able to overcome these impediments four important points must be borne in mind. First, any newcomer to an organization has to establish his credibility with and acquire the confidence of those whose work tasks and procedures are to be the subject of change. Senior management support needs to be clearly communicated to all levels of the organization. Second, the appropriateness of the outside agent's approach needs to be understood. As we have seen, different approaches may be required in different circumstances, and some, but not all, consultants are concerned with supplying one particular approach only. In this area it is difficult for client companies to make decisions since a principal reason for engaging the outside agent is often precisely a lack of expertise in this field. Third, the use of external agents of change does not negate the information-acceptability trade-off and its implications for the level of collaboration required. There is a danger that outside agents will attempt to hand down a solution from on high without involving individuals and work groups in the organization. Fourth, there is a need to ensure that the changes introduced are maintained after the external agent is no longer present.

Conclusions

Managing the introduction of IT involves consideration of external and internal factors. External factors involve the potential strategic gains arising from IT's contribution to improving the organization's competitive position. Internal factors concern the manner in which strategic objectives are carried out at the tactical and operational levels. The nature of change required by the introduction of IT was seen to raise issues about the appropriate types of organization structure and management style. These factors were shown to be firm-specific and, whatever the particular situation, related to improving the integration of the organization's activities. The following chapter extends the discussion and develops a means by which organizations can develop their own IT perspective.

References

D. A. Buchanan and D. Boddy, *Organizations in the Computer Age*, Gower, 1983.

J. Child, 'New Technology and Developments in Management Organization', *Omega*, Vol. 12, No. 3, 1984. (N.B. *Omega* Vol. 12, No. 3 was a special issue on the Impact of New Technology on Production.)

K. Davis, *Human Relations at Work*, 3rd edn., McGraw-Hill, 1967.

E. Jacobs, *et al.*, *The Approach to Industrial Change in Britain and Germany*, Anglo-German Foundation, 1978.

H. Koontz, C. O'Donnell, H. Weihrich, *Management*, Seventh Edition, McGraw-Hill, 1980.

F. Warren McFarlan, 'IT Changes The Way You Compete', *Harvard Business Review*, May–June 1984.

M. E. Porter, 'Please Note Location of Nearest Exit', *California Management Review*, Vol. XIX, No. 2, 1976.

D. J. Rhodes, M. Wright and M. Jarrett, *Computers, Information and Manufacturing Systems*, Holt, Reinhart, Winston, 1984.

D. Robey, 'Computers and Management Structure', *Human Relations*, Vol. 30, No. 11, 1973.

M. Thomson, 'Does IT Threaten Managers?', *The Director*, October 1984.

C. A. Voss, 'The Management of New Manufacturing Technology', *INRIA Conference on Production Systems*, Paris, April 23–26, 1985.

B. Wilkinson, *The Shopfloor Politics of New Technology*, Heineman, 1983.

4 IT and the integration of activities

Introduction

The previous two chapters aimed to provide insights into the nature of change and how to deal with it, on the one hand, and how the management of the introduction of IT should be geared to the circumstances faced by a particular firm, on the other. This chapter extends the general discussion to the detailed factors which influence policy and the methodology of introducing IT. We try to define how a company may determine its own specific needs and bring about change. In particular, we address the principal goal of introducing IT in an organization—to improve overall performance. The discussion in the previous chapter indicated that a desirable means of achieving this is by better integration of the organization's activities and functions. Integration, however, is in practice not well understood, being much talked about but difficult to define, let alone achieve. We examine how computer technology has been introduced in companies over the past two decades and to see what lessons may be learned in order to identify just what is to be integrated. The problems in achieving integration then are clearly related to the particular type of product offered, to the market addressed by an organization and to the discrepancies which may exist between the different types of information required by individual managers performing different functions. Overcoming these problems and selecting the appropriate type of technology may be achieved by seeking answers to a set of questions which diagnose the actions most appropriate to the organization.

How IT happens—stages of development

Large companies are more experienced than small ones and generally further up the 'learning curve' when it comes to understanding IT and its implications. They have been able to buy computers for 20 years and the cheap computers and other IT products of today are simply exposing the majority of companies to issues that these larger companies faced several years ago. The range of IT products is, of course, more extensive now; they are more 'user friendly' and need fewer specialists to operate them. Nevertheless, what has occurred in many of the larger organizations is a useful starting-point to examine the changes.

In the Harvard Business Review, Nolan describes the innovation of computers for data processing and information, across a sample of American companies. Table 4.1 shows the six stages of growth he has identified and the company diagram shown in Figure 4.1 provides a framework for discussion.

At stage 1 the company decides to install a computer. For obvious reasons the usual starting-point is financial where there is a great deal of paperwork and masses of data; everyone accepts this as something which computers can manage. Financial systems are mostly standardized. They are also disciplined for reasons of security and because of legislation about company bookkeeping. Additionally, the culture in companies in the United States and United Kingdom is such that financial managers tend to have control over initiatives. The office environment in which they work is close to the centre of authority and is somehow thought to be the natural habitat of computers, so 'high tech' innovation tends to start in finance. Once installed the computer invites reaction by its very presence. Naturally other departments want computers, either as a matter of principle about not being 'left out', or because, as is likely, they have genuine applications to support. The process moves to stage 2. At this point there are alternatives for the

Table 4.1 Historical penetration of computers for data
processing

Stage 1   *Installation*: The first opportunities to use IT are agreed.
Computers are installed. There is a capital involvement
and commitment to at least one application.

Stage 2   *Contagion*: Other departments identify their IT needs
perhaps through encouragement from upper management
or by a general desire to get their share. The costs of IT
continue to rise. There is usually a lot of independent
development of systems and programs driven by local user
enthusiasm.

Stage 3   *Control and containment*: At this point a variety of user-
oriented systems exist. They usually involve different
standards of programming. Their further development is
hampered by lack of data/information from other users
and yet they have neither the technical means nor program
compatibility to interconnect with them. Management
impose controls and attempt to rationalize the systems.
There is a move towards a formal system-management
function. Database systems and more central control of
computers is effected. Costs continue to rise and the
development of user applications is in temporary stagnation.

Stage 4   *Integration*: With a sound infrastructure of databases and
computers the user applications enter a new phase of
development. However, users have to be more accountable
for their use of, what by now is, a significant investment.

Stage 5   *Administration*: Users can draw on the database source and
are less concerned with hardware and software administration. The responsibility for the maintenance and security
of databases, the basic resource of most users, becomes an
important task. Emphasis is on administrating the data and
information system. Users now share data and are accountable for using it.

Stage 6   *Maturity*: The fundamental operational activities are confi-
dently established with reliable links to all the management control functions. It is possible to use the integrated
system for strategic purposes such as planning and
resource management. The emphasis at this point is on the
management of the corporation and its resources. The
maintenance of a healthy IT system is necessary to achieve
that end.

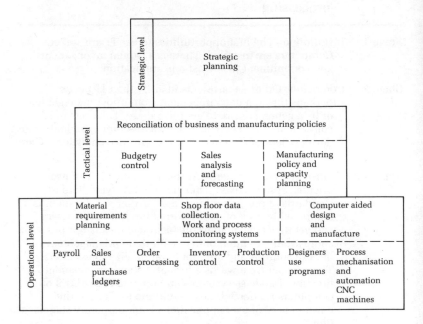

Figure 4.1 Hierarchy of integration at various levels in a (composite) company

company and its general style of management. Does it opt for tight management control or for a degree of operational 'slack'.

Control implies proceeding with a tight hold on the managerial reins. The initiative is kept at the centre of computing with new applications allowed only when cases are proven. Slack, on the other hand, involves letting initiative pass to the would-be users, allowing them to explore opportunities. A form of controlled flexibility is most usual; indeed, it is probably the only way to achieve the across-the-company experience necessary for the future exploitation of computers within a reasonable time scale, such as the lifetime of the initial installations. The costs of such broadening of applications are, of course, significant.

The transition from stage 2 to stage 3 may be difficult. Companies are sometimes unprepared for the continuing costs during the contagion phase. Some managers give too little attention to the original projects which then go awry and are disappointing. Technical problems and poor analyses of hardware requirements confound others. Changes in organization and even personnel are often necessary to cope with new ways of doing things. This takes time and can clearly lead to difficulties. There may be a reaction to the delays and the temporary uncertainty that innovation brings: too much control is then imposed and initiatives are suppressed. Stagnation and even withdrawal from any kind of involvement with IT can easily result.

Stage 3 is a rich phase in which the financial applications begin to realize that their source data are mostly distributed throughout the company in the form of order books, inventories, work-in-progress lists, shop-floor transactions and despatch notes, etc., etc. Production find that they are duplicating the data Sales have already entered in either their own computer or their share of the company's. What is worse, the version they have is slightly different, and neither version agrees entirely with the one held in Finance! The proliferation of ideas and understanding is impeded by incompatible though pertinent approaches. Efforts thus become directed towards uniformity, data sharing and technical integration in general. To be viable some of the autonomy of users is passed to the data processing department or central management. Expenditure on data processing continues with no further increase in the type of applications. Administering what already exists becomes an explicit goal. The computer systems adopt database methods. There is a change in emphasis from installing and controlling computers to data and database management during this stage. It is an important transition. Control rather than flexibility is needed to effect it.

The consolidation phase prevents the users from pursuing their locally perceived needs and opportunities.

Just when they are losing faith, the database option begins to bear fruit and they can not only pursue their ideas, but pursue them efficiently. By stage 4 the rationalized infrastructure is geared to their needs and they can share learning now based on common experience with the same basic methods and technology. Costs nevertheless continue to accrue as applications development recommences.

Stages 5 and 6 are less clearly defined because, as McNenney and McFarlan reported in 1982, few firms have proceeded beyond stages 2 or 3. Despite advances in information technology since that date, this is very much still the case in 1985, because of the issues discussed in this book. The administration of the data and information system infrastructure must itself be consolidated. A balance must be struck between the users and the administrators: a balance between control and flexibility, between stimulating user-oriented initiatives and stability.

As integration improves so does confidence. Management's understanding of the relationship between data and real activity improves and there is consistent rather than opportunistic exploitation of data. Data becomes acknowledged as a seriously valued resource and is used to manage the other corporate resources. Stage 6 is the culmination of steady evolution from small, operationally oriented applications, through management control to strategic planning and policy making.

The practical corporate significance of IT seems to have been acknowledged only after considerable periods of operational and tactical activity, not from a strategic perspective as would be ideal. In addition, the time-scale for implementing IT is longer than computer salesmen would have us believe. Employees *and managers* have to learn, not just new procedures but how to develop and explore the wider opportunities that IT systems afford.

Companies seem to be drawn into IT by the initiatives of opportunist (entrepreneurial) sub-departments. Corporate strategies appear to be a consequence rather than a source of such initiatives, although more recently 'integration' has begun to emerge as a recognizable issue in corporate policy making. Companies are now beginning to contemplate integration as a positive goal in which IT plays an important part. Twenty years of experience allow identification of specific issues and a reasonably precise approach to the introduction of IT and the creation of change. This means more confidence and clearer purpose, which increase the probability of success. What then is integration and how is it reconciled with different kinds of organization?

Integration and manufacturing systems

In organizational, functional and information terms, manufacturing companies are complex. They are a challenge, a prime candidate for IT and worthwhile and generalizable systems for integration. A manufacturing system is occasionally described as a "synthesis of men, materials, money and machines". The synthesis requires a lot of skill and the recognition that information and procedures are critical. All companies are integrated in the sense that they are the sum of their parts, but now integration means something more: the use of IT to bring about particularly successful synthesis.

In a manufacturing system the purpose of this 'improved' integration may be regarded as the successful control of operational slack; that is control of the delays, of the levels of stock and of the spare capacity. Some operational slack is always necessary to cover mismatches in what the company planned and what actually occurs. Unpredictable events invariably arise and will always thwart plans to some extent. In situations that vary the sequence in which manufacturing processes are carried out, slack makes a considerable difference to the utilization of plant, to the lengths of queues and the rate of output. Precise timetabling for a whole plant is difficult except in simple flow situations, and slack in some form is essential. One purpose of the information system is to reveal where slack is, to help hold it in the right quantity in the right places, to enable the organization to meet its corporate objectives effectively.

Integration is a term which has tended to be used very loosely. It can be classified into five types:-

Type 1: Goals-oriented

This is integration of goals within an organization. In systems theory the definition of a system requires that the parts have a common goal, against which the performance of the system as a whole is judged. On this definition few manufacturing companies have a manufacturing system, but rather a collection of systems concerned with different tasks and based on different disciplines with different perspectives.

Type 2: Functional

This 'vertical' integration covers 'hard' automation in terms of materials handling and process control automation, and also integration through computer software control in which decision-making has been embedded, in deterministic algorithms. Links between CAD and CAM are in this category, as are intelligent robots. In fact any combination of man and technology geared to integrating the flow of material from design conception to finished output could be said to be integrated in this sense.

Type 3: Planning and control

This is 'horizontal' integration which covers organizational structure and management practice by planning and control. It depends on the extent to which the planning of manufacturing operations is made explicit and debated by the various functions within the organization. It also includes the way the amount of slack in the organization is measured for comparison to the corporate policy goals.

Type 4: External

External integration refers to the strength of the links between the organization and the external environment. These may be strong in highly developed industries or where there are common technical standards or where commercial practice dictates. These highly developed systems are usually organized around key materials, major processing plant or large markets, e.g. coal, oil, chemicals, power generation, defence industries, medical supplies.

Type 5: Information infrastructure

Technical integration of IT is the extent to which information transmission is integrated in terms of data structure and physically controlled information or data transfer (computer/communications/networks). Information technology will not automatically lead to any of the other types of integration but it is probable that it will ultimately help them all. At present, the emphasis on equipment and the more objective methods of system design required to get the technology operating technically is tending to lead to an understatement of overall purpose and to other types of integration being neglected.

Organizations and integration

Organizations are necessary to support the process of synthesis discussed in the previous section, fundamentally as a consequence of the division of labour discussed in Chapter 3. Figure 4.2 illustrates a simple manufacturing system as a number of activities or subsystems. As we have seen in Chapter 3, ideally a manufacturing company would have a

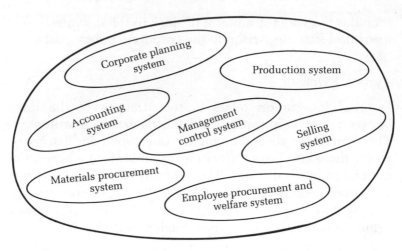

Figure 4.2 Simple systems representation of a manufacturing company

corporate objective which, re-defined in appropriate terms for each subsystem, would ensure that the efforts of each were directed to the same singular goal. In the system hierarchy one of the subsystems would be responsible for defining of subsystems objectives, in practice, probably the management control system.

Unfortunately, many commercial organizations do not have very clear objectives beyond the general ones of making a profit and surviving. Frequently, conceptual subsystems and the actual division of labour do not coincide. For example, the selling subsystem in Figure 4.2 may well involve contributions from the departments concerned with accounts, production, test, advertising and despatch as well as sales. An individual working in the accounts department may not understand this distinction, so the objectives of selling and of accounting become associated more with the ambitions of the sales and accounting departments and are inclined to be parochial. Departmental interests, subsystem goals and company objectives thus need to be nurtured to achieve true integration. Matrix management, referred to previously, is an attempt to satisfy this need to reconcile the systems of Figure 4.2 with, for example, the organization of Figure 3.4. Information technology can easily precipitate organizational problems by supporting the function but not the responsibility, e.g. performing selling functions outside the control of the Sales Department.

Whether or not their goals are clear, the operational activities of most organizations, e.g. what they make, what processes are involved, how many customers and so on, have an apparent purpose. The purpose determines the kinds of problem that arise particularly in relation to integration and IT. Figure 4.3 illustrates four different systems of activity, including the interactions with their customers. They are simplified representations of the banking system, the health service and two types of manufacturing company, A and B, and may be distinguished in three ways:

1. Whether the supplier or customer is dominant in defining the product.
2. The number of activities or processes potentially involved in the provision of the product.
3. The number of different, simultaneous demands per process on the company's capacity.

Banks define the products (services) they offer. For the bulk of dealings with the average domestic customer these are a small range of variations on withdrawing and depositing money. The physical processing is very small and the transactions are essentially the product. Computers identify, record and carry out the transactions almost instantaneously. Little discretion is required and is mostly covered by rules which are simple enough for some depositing and withdrawing transactions to be handled by machine (cash dispensers). The records of all transactions are processed in a central computer which provides simple aggregates of the Bank's total activity, virtually on request. This allows the Bank to pursue its principal objective,

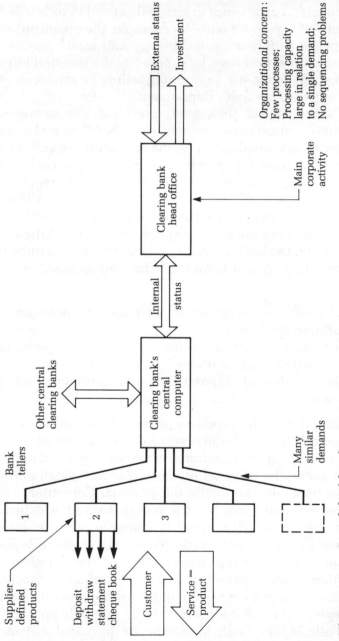

Figure 4.3a Simplified banking system

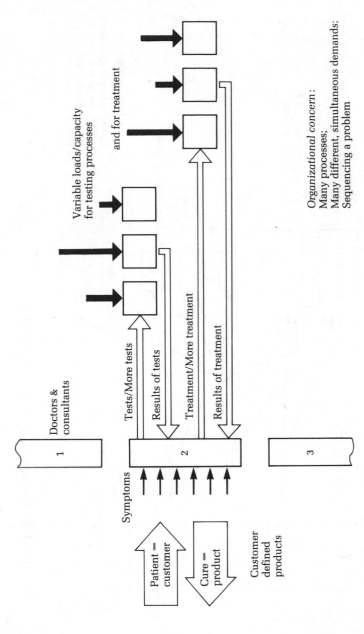

Figure 4.3b National health service

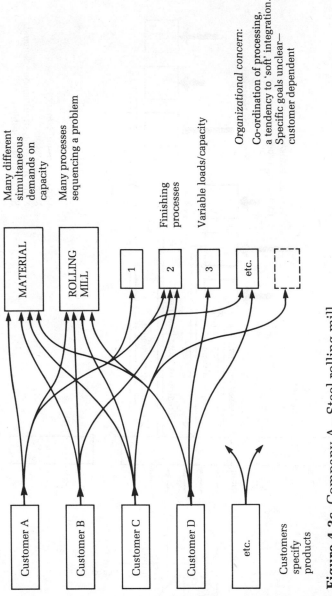

Figure 4.3c Company A—Steel rolling mill

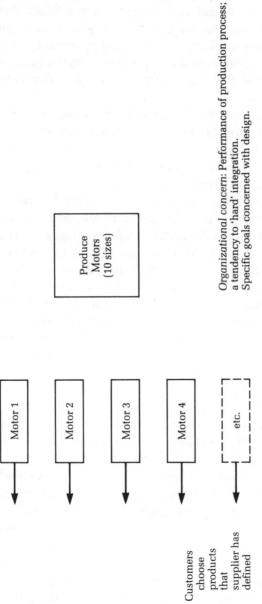

Figure 4.3d Company B—motor manufacturer

which is to invest the deposited money with a high rate of return. The central computer is a reference for how its internal operations are going, and, provided it has enough able people examining the external opportunities for investment, this is the best it can do. Slack in the banking system appears to be the money not yet invested that is truly available to invest.

The (nationalized) Health Service, at the doctor-consultant-hospital level, is in great contrast to the above. A patient (customer) arrives at the doctor (supplier) with symptoms from possible causes which can theoretically combine in millions of different ways. The patient wants a cure (product) but has no idea what it is (the specification of requirements). So judgement is needed to convert the symptoms into a diagnosis and the diagnosis into a treatment specification. In some cases the diagnosis will depend on some investigative work which must also be specified. These specifications across the whole Health Service produce many simultaneous demands for different skills and resources, the actual demand for any one skill or resource being largely unpredictable, particularly for the rarer diseases. The demand is, of course, determined none the less by the customer. To meet the requirements is difficult and a challenge. Practical systems cope by using very able people at the customer/supplier interface, e.g. doctors and consultants, and by organizing the resources (hospitals and specialist units) into semi-autonomous units with well-defined, local objectives 'to clear their queue within a simple framework of priorities'. The doctors and consultants thence book the patients into the resource units as demand and priorities allow. It may take several years to process certain types of patient in this way, yet the resources are fully used and the doctors and consultants are always busy. The operational slack is taken up in the form of delays for the customer. (Note: the private sector avoids delays and competes by transforming slack to the resources instead, adjusting prices to fine-tune demand to match capacity!).

Commercial Company A is a company which rolls special steels to order. It is essentially selling the processing capacity of its mill, a very expensive capital item, and a range of twenty or so different finishing processes, any five of which are usually required by a particular batch of steel. Customers define the product: the metallurgy of the steel, ingot weight, rolled size, quantity and quality of rolled lengths, annealing and finishing processes, bundling and mode of transport. They may also wish to dictate batch sizes, call-off rate and delivery date, though these are usually negotiated to some extent. The company's principal skill (the customer (and we) assumes he is competent at processing the order) is in establishing effective cost of individual orders within the context of the aggregate demand, without disappointing the customer. Slack occurs as work-in-progress lies around without progressing, or as unused, idle capacity or as delays to the customers.

Commercial Company B specializes in flameproof, alternating-current, electric motors. They supply the coal industry and oil industry for use in areas where explosions are a possible hazard. The products are made in 10 sizes, on a scale of power ratings, from 4 kW to 120 kW. The company has thus specified its product, and, although it responds primarily to customer orders, it has a make-to-stock, deliver-to-order option if it chooses, for all or some motors. Aside from the irrevocable basic choice of product and market, the company's prime skill is in making motors as cheaply and competitively as possible in the volumes it is likely to sell. It can choose its own terms for specifying, designing and making them. Employing the best techniques and appropriate machinery, its main strategy is to keep abreast of what such techniques and machinery might be by evaluating new ideas and costing alternatives. Slack, in an operational sense, can occur as spare capacity or excessive levels of stock. This should arise less than in Company A because there are very few combinations, the patterns of work are more predictable and more within the company's own power to control. Operational slack is more likely to be a creeping affair of inefficient processing, design obsolescence or overlooking external factors, for example changes to flame-proofing standards and legislation.

The above examples can be compared as in diagram Figure 4.4, which allocates the distinguishing features to three dimensions, each representing a (crude) scale of degree. In their simplest form the Bank and Health Service lie at the extremities. (Some aspects of both lie elsewhere but the illustration is generally valid and helpful.) Companies A and B lie within, and so do most other commercial organizations. The attempt to place a company at the correct point in the diagram is an important part of IT innovation methodology and focuses attention on the relative

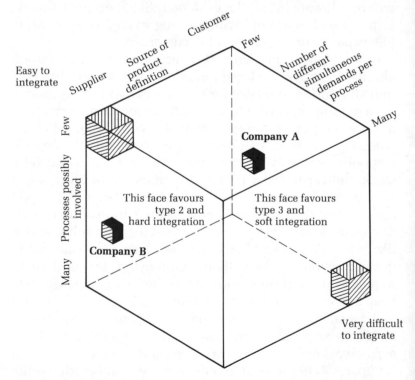

Figure 4.4 Organization features and integration

potential for type 2 and type 3 integration. As may be seen from the diagram, the type of activity described for the National Health Service produces serious difficulties for integration, whilst the opposite applies to banking activities. The developing revolution in personal financial services, in which IT plays a very important part, tends to confirm this view. Though Companies A and B lie within the two extremes it is necessary to appreciate that the types of integration involved are different. Company B favour Type 2 or hard integration. Company A favours Type 3 or soft integration. It is with this latter type of integration that the more serious management control issues may arise, since co-ordination is required across activities, rather than within an activity. The next section deals with these issues.

People and integration

Chapter 3 presented a review of the current understanding of human behaviour in organizations. This reviewed different management styles which might be used in different circumstances and in dealing with resistance to change by managers and employees in the organization. Although the importance of an agent for change was emphasized, it was also evident that where such a catalyst did not or could not possess all the necessary information, some element of collaboration was necessary. Without collaboration, resistance would probably result.

Where integration of different activities with different areas of responsibility is involved, varying types of information held by different people raise problems that need to be recognized and dealt with through some form of collaboration.

Managers, like everyone else, hold their own points of view and expectations determined by background, education, experience, job role, and personal prejudices. The job role offers quite a lot of variety in itself and the set of management roles in a company produces a variety of ways of viewing what are inherently the same activities. Differences are often most explicitly differentiated in information and are thus critical for IT. For example, the designer needs dimensions and graphical representations; whereas those responsible for materials procurement and purchasing require only the type number and volume. Maintenance engineers want to know the history of plant, faults and repairs; whereas accountants want to know prices and utilization and where to allocate costs. Production managers are concerned with lead times of products; accountants with accounting periods. Table 4.2 contains a list of typical specializations (points-of-view) and the appropriate units of measure and functional representations.

Responsibilities are another matter and transcend specialist functions or activities. In practice, though, responsibilities may be poorly defined; for example, the maintenance engineer and the purchasing manager can both be responsible for 'getting the product through the door' or for 'saving money' or for 'being more efficient'. However, incompatibilities may exist between each of these responsibilities and between the attempts of managers in each department to carry out any of them.

For integration to be achieved which improves overall performance, responsibilities need to be formulated for the organization as a whole which then feed down to individual functions in a consistent manner. General responsibilities can essentially be expressed in terms of models as shown in Table 4.3.

In practice, companies are inclined to pursue one model at a time in turn, in a dynamic pursuit of overall excellence. The concept of operational slack is also relevant here. Whether the slack is lodged with customers in the form of delayed delivery or high prices, or with the company in some form of inefficiency (excessive costs, capacity or stock) the particular measures should clearly be expressed in the information system. Information technology provides

Table 4.2 Representations of managers' points-of-view in relation to manufacturing function

Specialism	Unit of Measure	Representation
Accounts	Money	Profits cash flow
Sales	Order volume, delivery period (lead time)	Orderbook, analysis, product movements
Works	Output units (standard hours per hour)	Output, process utilisation, material flow
Purchasing	Volume of purchase orders	Requirement in relation to stocks and orderbook
Production Engineering	Process characteristics	Routings, process complexity
Design	Dimensions numbers of items, performance figures numbers of modifications	Graphical, design procedures
Quality Control	Tests, failure rates	Standards, procedures
Maintenance	Number of faults	Maintenance schedules, plant performance records
Production Control	Process capacity, (in same units) orderbook load	Process, orderbook status, priority lists

the opportunity to obtain and display operational status in a way which reflects:

1. Specialist, functional status and requirements—units of measure—representation.
2. Prime responsibility—recognition of models—provision to indicate slack—recognition of need to co-operate with other specialists.

In translating the conceptual idea of integration into a practical reality which utilizes IT, the perspectives of the managers in the organization must be reconciled with those of the expert charged with the installation of the technology. The managers and information technologists are by training and attitude likely to be some distance from each other. The common ground is the task before them, but there is little common language or philosophy to facilitate

Table 4.3 Different views of responsibility expressed as models

Advantages	Model (point of view)	Weaknesses
Simple aggregates Suitable for strategic decisions Direct relationship to survival and the interest of banks, shareholders and market confidence	Emphasise P + L Profit and loss (please the owner)	Accounting periods not related to manufacturing timescales Aggregates mislead connections between physical and operational performance Simplistic view of resources and their use
Making the best use of resources must be fundamentally good	Emphasise Efficiency (Use the resources, please production and the accountant)	You can always make good use of resources by foregoing consideration of the customer, e.g. do the work needed to keep machines busy rather than that to complete orders
Pleasing the customers must be fundamentally good	Emphasise Effectiveness (Deliver the goods, please Sales and the customers)	This passes control to the customers and resources are used inefficiently

communication. This is a difficulty for all managers, particularly incumbent managers going through the experience for the first time, if only because the technologist will normally have been through it all before! The responsible manager must thus attempt to identify and explore the opportunities between the mechanistic, transaction-handling activities with which the computers will invariably start, and the corporate and decision-making functions he should by duty understand. If he does not, who will? Is the visiting technologist either able, suitable, or foolish enough to determine the corporate decision-making role of the computer in a company which is not his own?

As the person most concerned with the detail of change, the technologist needs to be aware of all the information agents involved in the changeover process. But it becomes a formidable and time-consuming task for the agent to attempt to define all the information requirements himself. From what has been said about the nature of change and the possession of information it would also be a futile task. Possession of information by those who occupy particular roles provides an element of power. Attempts to remove the information held threaten the power holder, and consequently can arouse resistance.

The concept of an integrating team thus emerges, and this involves the following three kinds of people in the organization:

- managers, who are decision-oriented and take responsibility;
- operational personnel, who are transaction- or task-oriented;
- information technologists, who are responsible for installing the system.

Integration and technology

The information infrastructure type of integration (type 5) is exemplified by advertisements which offer computers and terminals against a background of apparently super-efficient offices. Each office contains a terminal and telephone line and each is connected to central computers and to other terminals. The images convey a strong sense of unification, but for the reasons already discussed here integration cannot be attributed to the technology alone. For any particular organization the technology probably exists to support such interconnections, but the computer system is relatively indivisible and, by its nature, the organization it is intended to support is purposefully subdivided.

Nevertheless, any reputable computer supplier should be able to supply a machine capable of data processing and word processing and communicating via a telephone line or direct link with other computers or terminals. For integration purposes, the technology is thus already available to meet the range of likely requirements. Centralization or non-centralization appears to be a common issue, for the reasons discussed in Chapter 3. It makes little difference to the capabilities of the computer system itself whether it is based on a central computer with many remote terminals or on a network of small computers. But in a smaller organization, and increasingly, even, in larger ones, the choice between a centralized and a non-centralized system has important implications for the running of the organization. A central computer involves a central staff, which offers empire-building possibilities and the inefficiencies which that may bring. Whilst this might have been unavoidable with earlier technology, it is less so today. Moreover, though a central-ized computer function may appear to give enhanced control, this can be illusory if such an approach is out of touch with what is really going on. A network involves the dispersed local users in more responsibility towards data security, but they will also feel more involved. The company will thereby have among its staff a large number of people who can help each other. In a smaller organization this aspect may be very important. Networks have the advantage of facilitating staged growth and an energetic individual, responsible for IT in a smaller organization, can co-ordinate the efforts of the users in applications areas and effectively run a data processing service without a special department. Anyone who has written software for a wide cross-section of business applications knows that the complexity of a system is roughly proportional to the product of the numbers of:

- users or people involved
- departments affected
- different transactions
- different reporting periods

However, once the data is captured the reporting aspects of any system are technically easy. (Though finalizing the definition of a report is very often a difficult matter.)

Operational-level systems such as order processing, MRP (material requirements planning), production planning and work-in-progress monitoring are complex, much more so than basic ledgers which involve fewer departments and people. To produce a financial summary for an operational-level system is easy. To extend a basic financial system (ledgers, order book and wages) to operations is extremely difficult. If learning is necessary, as Nolan's discussions suggest, there is more to be learned at the operations level than elsewhere. The conventional wisdom is to maintain a central database of well chosen files and data structures from the various transactions that occur throughout the organization and draw upon it for reports etc. However, getting the structure and content of the database right at the outset is difficult and adding to it later is complex. The form of database is the essence of the problem rather than a solution. If the database is well structured the re-design and evolution of reports over a period of time should not pose too many problems. The 'if' is a big one, because it depends on thinking through the issues raised in this chapter.

A methodology for achieving integration

There are methods for fomulating corporate strategy in general, using experienced consultants as catalysts in corporate debates about traditional issues of finance, legislation, markets, business getting, manufacturing policy and so on. There are also well-developed, even alternative techniques for specifying computer systems. Many of these are called system design methods, but the 'system' referred to is primarily the technical requirements of the computer. Most of these techniques break the system into entities, i.e., 'things' or nouns, and activities, i.e., 'actions' or verbs, and map the relationships which normally tie up to various 'business processes'. IBM's Business Systems Planning methodology defines a business process as 'groups of logically related decisions and activities required to manage the resources of the business'. The SADT (structured analysis and design technique) is similar. The basic difficulty in applying these approaches comes when the goals of the system are not clear, which is the case with the kinds of manufacturing system which require type 3 integration.

A requirements specification for an information system is simply not readily obtainable because firstly the current methods of operation are difficult to understand due to their complexity, and secondly, the operating flexibility required for type 3 activities means the method of operation is continuously changing.

Possibly the only general approach which bridges the methodological gap is the Checkland method (Figure 4.5). This involves the identification of 'human activity systems' as systems held together by common perspectives on issues and tasks amongst the participants. An essential part of the method is the establishment of the minimum root definition which comprises the transformation process in the system, the owner (i.e. the agency with prime concern for the system and power to cause the system to cease to exist), the actors (i.e. those affected by the system), and the environmental constraints. It attempts to resolve the problems associated with points-of-view and to reconcile different models (Table 4.2). The approach uncovers the real purposes of systems and clarifies the role of the participants, but tends to lead to a redesign of the entire manufacturing system around the transformation process (manufacturing or principal activity) and the goals. In the manufacturing environment being considered here, the method often proves to be too fundamental and remote for initial use. Because of the way organizations deal with change, it implies an amount of disruption which, if attempted all at once, would cause considerable difficulties. The inherent danger may then be that bad experience with an initial attempt at introducing IT may produce reluctance to pursue the issue further.

A more practical approach, which builds upon rather than replaces the existing system, and which includes more

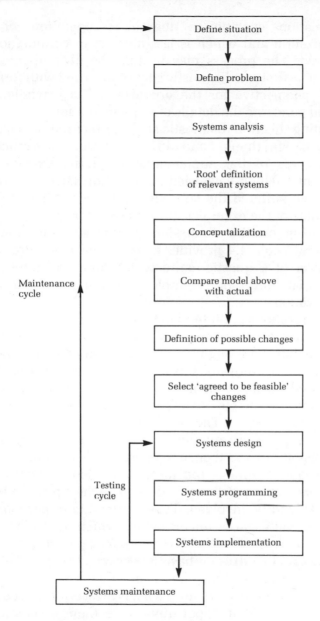

Figure 4.5 Checkland methodology applied to systems development and analysis cycle

information specific to the basic operation of the organization and which is less abstract in connotation, is required. The process may usefully be divided into two parts. The first is a diagnostic stage concerned with forming an IT perspective for the organization as a whole. The second concerns the details of implementation.

Getting this first diagnostic stage correct requires a great deal of careful thought and difficult decisions. It is crucial to the success of the implementation phase. Examples of companies which have tried to take short-cuts around this stage and suffered the consequences are not hard to find (see some of the examples given in Chapter 5).

Drawing on the discussion in this and the previous chapters, Table 4.4 provides a structured methodology in the form of a questionnaire which aims to identify the appropriate form of IT implementation for a particular organization.

The questions are intended to force issues into the open, to identify a company's position. There are no 'right' answers but there ought to be some kind of answer before the would-be innovator sets out to innovate. The questions are based on a systematic application of the points discussed in this chapter against a background of the theories in Chapters 2 and 3. They are linked in a conceptual framework which is essentially 'top down', from purpose to responsibilities and thence to operational support.

Question 1 applies the ideas contained in Figure 4.4. Answers to this question will determine the types of integration likely to be involved. Type 3 integration, particularly, will normally raise uncertainties which Question 2 is designed to resolve. What is the corporate position and what emphasis or blend of emphasis is necessary to support it? The models in Table 4.3 must be included, but for an individual firm it is necessary to identify what is most critical to corporate interests. What opportunities are there to communicate them with appropriate emphasis and responsibilities in an IT system? Question 3 should begin to resolve this by

Table 4.4 Questions to form an IT perspective and innovation methodology

Q1.	What business are you in?	• Nature and number of processes involved • Relative emphasis of product definition; customer or supplier • Nature of demand • Basis of competition • Form of integration most relevant
Q2.	What points-of-view have most bearing on the way you define responsibilities and run the business?	• Profit-and-loss model • Effective penetration of the market • Efficient use of company resources • Blend of the above
Q3.	Can you identify the information requirements in relation to your particular company and its market?	• The specialist managers must define their 'ideal' requirements, e.g. materials procurement, production control, etc. and explain the areas of uncertainty and required flexibility
Q4.	Are they consistent with the answer to Q1?	• Check
Q5.	Can you reinforce the points-of-view with information from IT equipment and make sense of the technological opportunities and relate them to functions in your company?	• Check • Opportunities for communications, data processing, word processing • Centralised or networked
Q6.	Is your organisation capable of handling IT and the changes it infers?	• Employees can accommodate change • Understand concepts of management control and slack • Organization can accommodate changes in responsibilities • Slack resources available to accommodate changeover • Resources and skills available to deal with resistance
Q7.	Can you name someone to be responsible for the company's commitment to exploiting IT?	• Senior manager(s) capable of maintaining impetus of change over a long period. What is the agent for change?
Q8.	Can you decide in which area to initiate change?	• Depends on above answers
Q9.	Can you imagine the follow-up initiatives and estimate cost effectiveness?	• Check
Q10.	Can you manage the innovation?	• Check

highlighting the specialist functions. These in turn identify the information requirements which must be represented in the total system.

Questions 4 and 5 are checks. Are the answers so far consistent? Is a strong personality beginning to distort the overall picture by selfish pursuit of detail? Are the ideas capable of IT support? If not, why? Questions 6 and 7 are self-explanatory, but often overlooked. In any company some personification of the commitment to innovate is necessary. He may be the actual agent of change or simply supportive. If there is no prior experience of IT then it is probably foolish to proceed without creating a learning possibility, for example, some non-critical but not oversimplified part of the proposed application. This will serve to answer Questions 8, 9 and 10.

Given the practical difficulties which may be involved in dealing with sudden comprehensive change—the company has to stay in business during as well as after the change process—an appropriate starting-point has to be decided upon. Future stages of IT can then be introduced in phases. To managing the company must be added the possibly more difficult skill of managing innovation.

Combining Figure 4.5 and Table 4.4 a modified phased approach to the introduction of IT can be defined (Figure 4.6). After the initial implementation, monitoring involves both checking to see whether the IT deals with the specific problem that it was designed to remedy and also, at a more strategic level, whether the IT still fits with the perspective developed by the firm. In a changing environment, it cannot be assumed that the IT perspective developed initially will remain valid. Additionally, questions must be asked to check whether the introduction of IT worked sufficiently well first time round for the same means to be used for the next part of the implementation process. Not only is the introduction of IT a learning process, but the means by which it is introduced involve learning also. Assuming the firm has sufficient resources available to effect further change, the next area for the introduction of IT may be selected.

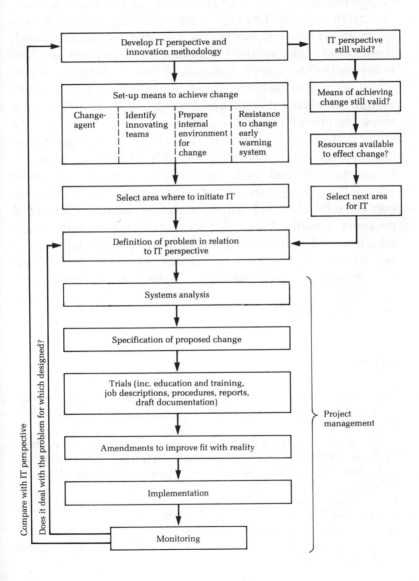

Figure 4.6 Staged approach to the introduction of IT

Conclusions

Achieving successful implementation of IT, where success means that the technology really is doing the job it was intended to do, is not easy. As this chapter has indicated, the process may usefully be divided into two parts: the first involves finding the IT perspective and making decisions about what is to be done, the second the detailed stages of systems analysis, design and introduction. The following three chapters address these two crucial parts using case study material to highlight the issues involved. Chapter 5 is concerned with the factors involved in finding a reasonable IT perspective and with the problems which may result where this is not carried out. Chapters 6 and 7 are concerned with detailed implementation issues. Chapter 6 presents a methodology for systems analysis and design which would enable the objective of integrating activities to be realized. Chapter 7 uses a hospital case study to highlight the important organizational and behavioural issues which can make the difference between successful and failed implementation.

References

A. S. Carrie and S. K. Banerjee, 'Approaches to Implementing Manufacturing Information Systems', *Omega*, Vol. 12, No. 3, 1984.

P. Checkland, *Systems Thinking, Systems Practice*, Wiley, 1981.

E. W. McFarlan, J. L. McKenney and P. Pyburn, 'The Information Archepelago—Plotting a Course', *Harvard Business Review*, January–February, 1983.

R. L. Nolan, 'Managing the Crises in Data Processing', *Harvard Business Review*, March–April, 1979.

A. T. Wood-Harper and G. Fitzgerald, 'A Taxonomy of Current Approaches to Systems Analysis', *The Computer Journal*, Vol. 25, No. 1, 1982.

5 Short cuts, partial successes and some failures

Introduction

The foregoing chapters have explored the issues most pertinent to effecting change in organizations through the introduction of IT. They have attempted to identify the problems in general terms and to indicate the kind of methodology that organizations should adopt to arrive at a strategy relevant to their individual needs. Nevertheless, such methodologies are not techniques which may be blindly followed. Skill and judgement are needed in applying them. This chapter is thus concerned with a number of real cases which, though somewhat simplified for clarity, illustrate the connections between theory and practice and some of the skills involved. Each case is presented in three parts: a description, a review of the methodology (so far as one can be detected) and an analysis of the changes produced by IT.

A case of blurring function and responsibility

Description

This example involved the group financial director of a large publicly quoted company to whom the board delegated the task of trying out microcomputers for management support. Wages and accounts were already computerized at head office. He decided to examine just one area of application and selected for attention one of the non-ferrous foundries in the group. This subsidiary was having problems with achieving delivery targets. Seemingly uncontrolled arrears led to the vicious circle of uncertain deliveries, crisis resolution of forced priorities, inefficient use of capacity, worse arrears and poor deliveries. He felt that a computer might help to provide more up-to-date information about the status of orders to help managers decide what jobs to do next. It might also give a clearer indication of committed load and spare capacity to help determine more realistic delivery targets without under-utilizing resources.

He started by examining the information in the problem area. The data for current orders and work-in-progress amounted to approximately 750 records, each containing details of a particular order including processes, process route, planned and actual dates and cost codes. It could thus be handled by a medium-sized microcomputer of approximately 1 Megabyte of floppy disc storage. He selected one of the several suitable machines available in this class on the basis of proven reliability, maintenance support and the availability of a database software package which made it immediately possible to maintain the status of current orders.

However, there were no programs for extracting the information needed to make the system into a management tool. Reporting programs were necessary to aggregate and review the status information for the specific purposes of the foundry. So he defined the reports and obtained a quotation for having programs written to extract reports from the database. The supplier agreed to supply the computer, database package and programs for just under £10,000 and an order was placed.

The reporting programs are of two types. One type aggregates the value of orders and work in progress by various categories such as product group, geographical area and sales representative. Value can be further subdivided into material and labour costs and sales value. This program was written and implemented within three months, and is used at monthly management meetings as a means of evaluating performance and directing sales. Figure 5.1 illustrates one such report.

Order number	Foundry costs				Non-foundry costs				
	Pattern	Core	Shell	Other	Ward 10	Ward 7	Drill	Material	Total
8648B	101			28	316	81		206	732
8579		180		50	280			130	640
8690		120	110	60		120	80	80	570
8691			90	85		216		20	411
8727	77				510			100	687
8515A	81			90			80		251
Total	259	300	200	313	1,106	417	160	536	3,291

Foundry material costs   494   Non-foundry material costs   536

Figure 5.1 *Valuation of work-in-progress*: Birmans stock valuation—work-in-progress and finished goods stock in units of 10p using Rate A as at 1 November 1982

The second type is concerned with the loading of orders onto processes in priority order of delivery date. The program computes for each day and each process, the orders to be processed on the shop-floor, for up to seven weeks ahead. This is done using finite capacity figures and rules like, 'not more than one operation or process per day per order'. The computed information is then used to produce work-to lists for each process and to list the load and free capacity by day and process. The latter is intended to help production to slot in new orders and support decisions on the issue of work to utilize free capacity and improve the accuracy of delivery promises. Figure 5.2 shows part of a schedule for some of the machine shop processes.

It was to be a year before the second type of report was operational at a further cost of £3,000 for programming because, after the first reports had been produced, the production controller pointed out that there were up to nine machines per process not one. This increased the size of the scheduling computation, exceeded the software capabilities and required a tenfold increase in processing time per schedule.

Orderload option 1: Day 45 to Day 50
Machine Shop

Day number	Milling order	Mins	Drill/Slt order	Mins	Grooving order	Mins	Fran'lube Order	Mins
45	8515A	560/0	8700	460	8513	510/0		
			8515C	595				
			8890	200				
46			8515A	1020				
47			8584C	105				
48					8584C	105/0	8515A	460/0
49	8616	140/0						
50			8616	85				

Figure 5.2 Short-term loading by machine centre

After much thought and some tension, the supplier, by employing special techniques, and the company, by accepting an all-night run every time they wanted a new schedule, managed to achieve the desired reports at an extra charge equivalent to the price of the original programming!

The scheduling reports were abandoned within a year and the company is currently installing a large central computer to handle all their systems.

Methodology

There is evidence of methodology, though not in the full meaning of the term as used in this book. The financial director was clearly the responsible and well-motivated agent for creating change, carrying authority and the commitment of the board. In selecting one area to tackle and in separating 'database' from 'reporting' functions he was objective and acting in accord with sensible practice. If the exercise were regarded as one of initiation or experimenting as in Nolan's stage 1 (Chapter 4) then it was a success. On the other hand there were clearly setbacks, which more attention to methodology might have avoided, and opportunities were probably missed. Using Table 4.4 as a guide, the following points emerge in response to the questions Q1 to Q10.

Q1.   The company is selling capacity and alternative routes through some of a wide choice of processes. There are many simultaneous demands for the same process. Type 3 integration (soft) is involved and the prime issue is co-ordination. How do they keep the customers happy while using the resources as fully as possible and profitably? .

In operational terms, the scheduling to finite capacity of jobs involving many operations together with processes handling several operations per day has not generally, from the years of experience with mainframe computers, been very successful. Process problems and general deviations from operational plans rapidly spoil the integrity of any schedule. It is thus rarely more than a guide for only a few operations ahead. To schedule, and re-schedule, for several weeks is likely to produce much unwanted paper and the general impression on the shop-floor that management does not know what it is doing. More fundamentally, scheduling is an attempt to turn the problem of type 3 integration into the easier flow-line, functional, type 2. The idea is a good one but it rarely works. Slack has to be introduced to allow for deviations and most practical schedules concentrate on displaying current availability of orders and process capacity. Within a framework of priorities and total load across processes, the foreman and shop-floor are usually able to use capacity very efficiently. If a clear picture of current and planned activity is not presented to those in charge, almost all schedules revert to processing 'that which is priority' or 'that which happens to be available'.

Q2, Q4.   Monetary value (profit and loss) and use of
           resources (efficiency) predominate which is con-
           trary to the observation in Q1 that the nature of
           the business is customer- rather than product-
           oriented. One would have expected the flow of
           orders (effectiveness) to be monitored as well.

Q3.   In Figure 5.1, sales are reported primarily by
           value, but the accumulation of reports over a
           period of time would, because they are categor-
           ized by salesmen, area and product, give some
           indication of market and sales performance *per
           se*. The schedules of Figure 5.2 are of use to sales
           only if they are actually achieved, which they are
           not. Support for future sales promises on delivery
           dates is absent. The computer could calculate the
           best possible date by re-running the scheduling
           program for each enquiry but that is impractical.
           Customers are not considered explicitly and if the
           schedule fails it is the customer who takes up the
           slack. A customer who perceived this fact would
           consider it a reason for concern.

Q5, Q6.   The computer schedule and reports are produced
           in the production control area (functional depart-
           ment) but clearly address matters of selling, pro-
           ducing and accounting. Thus the computer and
           system (IT) do not align with organizational
           responsibilities at an operational level, although
           the fact that only one area is immediately
           involved does facilitate initial training and assi-
           milation.

Q7, Q8.   The agent for change and the area of application
           are clearly identified.

Q9, Q10.   The use of IT seems to have been conceived by
           the financial director whose ideas predominate.
           There is no evidence of outside views or of a con-
           tribution from production and sales personnel.
           The system was conceived as a 'program' not as

an integrating influence and the wider implications of innovation and participation appear to
have been ignored.

Analysis

The changes in the company were potentially great but in
practice small. An obvious achievement is the increased
awareness at all levels of the reality of IT in the operations
area. Tangible outcomes are the improved records of sales
(Figure 5.1). However, the efforts of production control to
maintain a database provide little support for their own
operational decisions and mostly serve the sales performance reports. Function and responsibilities are blurred.
Future innovation must clearly be handled more slowly
with a strategy which allows several points of view to be
considered. A feasibility study would have resolved the
system requirements before the company committed itself
to the computer.

A Case where the system is there to serve the operations

Description

This example arose in a subsidiary company of a very large
organization, well known in engineering. The subsidiary
makes precision mechanical engineering components for
the nuclear industry. At the outset, it already had a data processing department and a computer for order processing,
payroll, inventory and general accounting purposes.

The board of this company decided to extend the computer installation. They called in the original supplier (A) to
install extra terminals and to write additional programs.
The purpose of this expansion was to enable the computer
to store the operations and routing sequences for all the

machine shop parts and assemblies and thereby to monitor work via shop-floor terminals. This would give them better disciplined and cheaper works records and cost data. A contract was placed with Supplier A who commenced work in a generally worthy and acceptable manner within these terms of reference.

But seeds of future discontent had already been planted, because the drive to obtain the works data came from the data processing manager and accounts department. Production control and the works manager were not thoroughly consulted. They believed that the scheme was of no fundamental use to them for improving the actual use of resources, without provision for load and capacity planning (probably true). However, Supplier A and the data processing manager agreed that the expansion would absorb the remaining capacity of the main computer and they would not look seriously at this further area.

Such was the frustration of the works manager that he started looking at small, general-purpose microcomputers to see whether anything was available to meet his requirements. He found a suitable machine available through Supplier B, which is not surprising since there is a wide choice in the appropriate class. More important, Supplier B was also prepared to write the special programs to the production controller's specification. The principal program involved taking all the items from the current order-book (parts and various levels of sub-assemblies) and from the lead time estimates and due dates supplied, to assign week numbers to each operation. It then calculated the load on capacity (by machine groups). Other programs listed items overdue and items already available at particular machines. Delivery is very important in this industry because delays can hold up work on major capital items and leave many people idle. The quotations in June 1982 were very modest, £6,000 for the computer and £3,000 for the programs.

With the quotations and support from the production controller, the works manager started to make a case for purchase. Grudging approval for the system was finally obtained from the board, 'provided it remained within the quoted costs and would really work'.

Representatives of the company visited two previous installations of Supplier B at the supplier's expense and had a further demonstration. Supplier B, with such increasing overheads was now desperate to close the sale but because of the pressure of his clients (the work's manager) and the shortage of money, was reluctant to re-negotiate an increase in price.

Six months had passed meanwhile and the deadline for Supplier A to complete the extension to the main computer was approaching. At a single meeting of Supplier B, the works manager and production controller, it was decided to proceed. But the production controller had by now studied the procedural and job description aspects of what he had specified and admitted some disquiet at the number of updating transactions with which he would have to deal.

At this same meeting the somewhat panicky suggestion that this small computer receive some data normally resident in the main computer was therefore voiced. It was consequently decided that a floppy disc containing a file of progress information should be produced each week by the main computer. This same disc would then be transferred to the small computer and the data read automatically. A few telephone calls to the manufacturers confirmed that this method was possible and that a standard program costing £200 was available to read the disc on the small computer.

An order was then placed with Supplier B on condition that the computer and programs were delivered within two months. The additional transfer program was purchased, from stock, from an agency.

Supplier B provided the computer and software on time. Tests with small files of 'example' data confirmed that transfer was possible and the principal planning and listing programs, after some minor adjustments, were accepted.

Supplier A was meanwhile three to four months behind with the extension to the main computer. The company were thus unable to test the small computer under full operating conditions. They paid the invoice. The three-month warranty on the computer and program support meanwhile expired. The company had also decided not to enter a maintenance agreement with suppliers in regard to the *small* system.

Upon attempting to run operationally, two practical difficulties arose.

The first occurred when the full-scale transfer by disc was attempted. The alignments of the disc drives on the main computer and the small computer were not consistent across the full disc of data. The program to read the data from the disc prepared by the main computer thus crashed sufficiently often to prevent operational use of the small one. This started a witch-hunt.

The data processing manager held himself not responsible. He had not been an advocate of this system anyway.

Supplier B had no funds left within the costs allotted to this sale to pay for further effort and was resolute about 'no further work without payment'. The works manager was angry and frustrated. The production controller had virtually what he wanted with the very lists that he had specified but they were never sufficiently current to be useful.

After much delay and acrimonious discussion within and outside the company the drives on both computers were re-aligned at the company's cost, well under £500. This reduced the occurrence of the fault and the system became operational.

It was at this point that the second problem arose. The specification had implicitly assumed that all items relating to a particular order would be available in the computer when the planning program was being used. Common sense would seem to decree that one cannot plan a complete job unless the complete requirements are known. Yet, because lead times for manufacture in this industry can extend to more than a year, some information about assembly details was, it transpired, often not available until part-way through the manufacturing program. This had not arisen in the previous manual system which had aspired to little pre-planning on the scale now envisaged. The result was that the computer correctly calculated loads but in the absence of these items they were operationally at the wrong dates.

A brief discussion between the production controller and the systems analyst of Supplier B revealed a practical solution based on a simple rule about lead time estimates that the production controller felt would be appropriate for missing items. But the essence of the program to be changed resided in the main algorithm for doing the planning. A change here would be delicate and the whole system would require careful re-testing to check that new errors had not been introduced. The scale of the work involved could easily approach 50 per cent of the original programming.

Further acrimony and an unsatisfactory compromise on price for Supplier B nevertheless provided a solution to this problem, six months after Supplier B had satisifed the original contract.

Methodology

Table 4.4 again provides guidelines for reviewing a case in which an explicit methodology is clearly lacking.

Q1.   The company is process oriented, selling capacity for many simultaneous demands on many processes in different combinations and sequences. Type 3 integration is of prime concern because of the co-ordination required to meet the customer specification and delivery dates. Type 5 integration is also important because the existing data processing department has a computer with links to several other departments already.

Q2.   The point of view of production planning and control was not taken fully into account at the outset. The data processing department was clearly more aligned with the accounting and works records functions (value monitoring) than with production control (order progress and process planning). Responsibility towards customers and product flow (effectiveness) were left to production control without IT support.

Q3.   Production's information requirement was either ignored or deemed a lower priority than other applications for the remaining capacity of the existing computer. Objectively the case was, however, strong and hence the late but definite decision to go ahead with a supplementary microcomputer.

Q4.   Production were supposed to integrate with the existing system on resources barely adequate for a simple stand-alone application. This application concerns a database containing all orders exploded to a level of detail which includes individual operations and process times for all parts, assemblies and orders. The report of load-on capacity, which uses a load to infinite capacity algorithm and is thus not a scheduling algorithm, involves computations several orders more difficult than those for budgets or wages calculations. Although the computer is small, the application is not.

Q5.   Communication with the existing computer turned out to be critically important. The method of communication was addressed late in the day and rather badly handled.

Q6, Q7, Q8.   Production were largely isolated with their

point of view and no one person with overall authority was interested in integration as such. (The production director eventually forced co-operation to achieve the technical integration of the existing and supplementary computers but there was no agent for change at the outset.)

Q9, Q10.   They were barely able to manage the innovation. It was achieved by a number of individuals, some of whom were coerced.

Analysis

The application is a major one affecting all issues of productive work and processing expenditure. It has a direct bearing on delivery performance in a delivery-sensitive industry. Yet, the corporate attitude seems to indicate: small computers, small system, small investment, little impact and little attention. The ultimately successful attempt to rectify the original oversight did not deserve to succeed, but is a credit to the tenacity of the enthusiasts in production control who felt that IT was an important tool which could support them.

If one were to approach a member of the company's board he would explain that all this is temporary and that they are looking for a 'system' at this moment from XYZ which is almost what they want to meet all their requirements. Of course they would need to be sure before they invest the £200,000 or so that it will cost and are looking into how the 'system' might be made more flexible. They have told the same story for each of the past four years. It is a genuine story. The truth is that they are not close enough to the detail in their own company to be able to compare systems with their needs nor do they have a methodology for tackling the problem of defining them. They will never make a decision except by chance. Packages are very, very unlikely to meet the needs of soft, type 3 integration.

CADMAT, an example of hard integration

In contrast to the previous two cases, this example is concerned with hard, type 2 integration. The company concerned makes telecommunications equipment to customer order in a basically simple range, including telephone exchanges and various kinds of transmitting and receiving apparatus. However, there are many variations. A telephone exchange is no longer a simple handset and switching facility. Modern exchanges must offer all the options like call logging, conferencing, queuing, transfers and call-back facilities, in any combination the customer might want. This means that a very large number of alternative combinations can arise, many of which require individual changes at the level of detailed circuit design. At least, that is how it is now. In the past, the complexity of such equipment was so great that customers and suppliers both accepted that options produced delays, high costs and unreliability. The market was content with a few standard products. But, the development of integrated circuits has literally encapsulated much of the complexity and the microprocessor has permitted greater flexibility through the use of software (programs) where previously circuits were necessary. Optional extras are now possible and competition in the market insists that suppliers not only offer them but can produce these customer-specified goods on time and at competitive prices.

Hard integration appears to be the solution and can best be explained in relation to Figure 5.3. This shows the concept of CADMAT or Computer Aided Design, Manufacture and Test. In the form shown it has not really been achieved anywhere as of today, but several companies are very close, including the subject of this case.

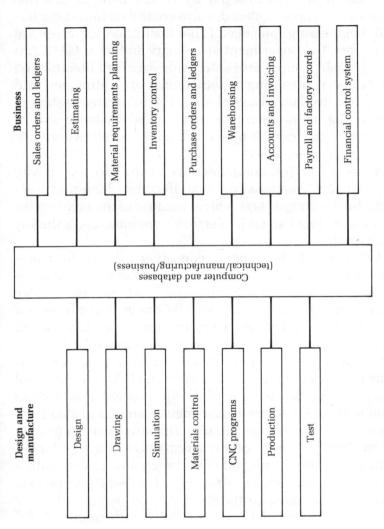

Figure 5.3 A hard, integrated system

Description

The activities most affected by IT are hard to describe because the opportunities devolve around technical matters and engineering practice. (The Institution of Electrical Engineers, the Department of Industry and most CADCAM and CADMAT suppliers can provide excellent literature on the subject including photographs of equipment and computer displays.) Nevertheless, the integrated system of Figure 5.3 is representative of typical systems and is relevant to this case. It operates broadly as follows with IT permeating every aspect.

A computer (or computers) is central to all activity whether for business or manufacture. Manufacturing includes the design stage which, because of the rapid evolution and major changes in electronic engineering, is the key to integration.

At the outset, the designer conceives a design for a product or to meet a customer specification. Design is supported by computer programs and special display screens which allow circuits to be drawn directly onto a VDU (visual display unit/computer terminal). Libraries of existing circuits and circuit elements are stored in the computer for reference, modifications or extension. New circuits can be added to this database which, over a period of time, reduces the amount of detailed design that is done from scratch. Customer requirements can be satisifed from combinations of proven circuits. Drawings can be printed automatically. The concept of a drawing office is no longer critical; drawing is integral with design and anyone with a display unit can view the 'drawings'. Imposing discipline is easy because access to the database can be controlled by password/authorization codes. The proliferation of different designs for similar tasks is thus avoided and consistent standards can be imposed on circuits and components.

Simulation in computer software has proved practical for many digital and some analogue circuits. The database of designs can be tested for performance by simulators so that prototyping is not always necessary to prove a design.

A ubiquitous item in electronic equipment is the printed-circuit board. The layout of its circuits and the location of the integrated circuits and components is computerized. From the database containing circuit diagrams, integrated circuits, component lists, pin connections and dimensions, programs produce 80 per cent or so of the printed-circuit board design. The remainder is achieved interactively with the help of a technician and visual display unit.

Once a design exists within the computer in terms of circuit definition, performance simulation, printed-circuit board layout, component and integrated-circuit lists, manufacture of the completed boards is achieved under program instruction. On request, the computer will automatically produce photomasters and drilling instructions for the printed-circuit boards. It will provide the programs which assemble kits of components and integrated circuits and insert them automatically into the boards.

Because the performance of the circuits are in the database it is also possible to probe and test the completed boards automatically. Faults are thereby identified during manufacture and the circuits are rectified or rejected.

All the manufacturing details are thus in the computer. By maintaining the business database, alongside them the internal implications of all current activity are, in principle, available to the company.

Methodology

The questions of Table 4.4 are again a useful guide.

Q1.   In high-technology companies like this one, the manufacturing activity is analogous to the craft manufacture of furniture. The basic processes of procuring wood, manufacturing the parts, assembling the item and finishing it are similar for all items. The same craftsman may be assigned to make chairs or tables and different kinds of chair or table. So too in CADMAT the processes are similar, but the variations in the products are catered for by programs encapsulating some of the designers' intelligence and particular requirements.

In principle, the company is customer-oriented selling capacity. Unlike the previous examples, however, the many simultaneous demands for processes are subject to two important simplifications:

- the sequence of processing is virtually always the same.
- setting-up times of processes are very short: they are often instantaneous, involving only the selection of a different computer program.

This means that the type 3 integration problems are reduced to the simpler, type 2, flow-line variety.

Q2.   There is a consensus in this part of the electronics industry that the approach is correct, that flow-line, hard-integration is efficient and effective. Thus equipment manufacturers, software houses and company employees need no longer speculate. They can direct their interests towards what is now an identifiable approach in need of refinement. The areas for corporate concern are:

- What is the state-of-the-art in design and how often do they re-design? (Design slack.)
- What are the trends in the market, customer requirements, new components, competitors' products?
- How do they manage materials procurement? Electronic components are expensive and the chances of obsolescence are high.

These are external, type 4 integration issues, which, being less tangible than the CADMAT hardware and software, are easily neglected.

Q3.   The domination of the design and manufacturing processes by computers and the tendency of technologists to prefer task-oriented methods means that the IT is readily accepted. However, the different specialists, for example 'design engineers' and 'production engineers', choose different suppliers for their needs. For example, the best system for printed-circuit board layout may be provided by company XYZ but the best methods of component insertion are provided by company PQR. Unfortunately, they may not be compatible with the rest of the system so the practical aspects of type 5 integration pose problems. Since the corporate investment in any one area is large the decisions are likely to affect activities and policy for several years ahead. The nature of the compromise is critically important.

Q5—Q9. The technologists in the organization appreciate the IT because it is representative of their own products, profession and interests. The agent for change is, on the one hand, their own awareness of technological progress and personal desire to be associated with it. On the other hand, the corporate need to survive is only fulfilled via hard integration. Obstruction by non-technologists is unlikely, since the numbers of employees in this category are diminishing, as integration and automation proceed.

Q10.   Managing the changes needed to arrive at the state described above is clearly a challenge. The objectives are clearly expressed in Figure 5.3, but the evolution is difficult. Companies like this one, seem to have gone through two phases and are entering the third and final one which is close to requirements.

Firstly, in the period up to about 1970, they used a conventional organization with many specialist departments and functions. The technology they used was labour intensive and the style of operation was characterized by man management and co-ordination difficulties. This phase continued into the era of printed circuits which reduced the amount of wiring, simplified a lot of the technical work and reduced the manpower requirements for a given scale of operation.

Secondly, the advent of integrated circuits (miniature circuits, often equivalent to a printed-circuit board) reduced the size of equipment, and the amount of technical detail per product. Coincidentally, the same technology produced the microprocessor and microcomputers. Cheaper computers increased the range and use of computer-controlled machines and permitted the development of programs to assist with design. The co-ordination of manufacturing tasks became simpler with four processors and people to manage. Specialist departments were left to develop local opportunities and suppliers sprang up to compete for potential business in CAE, CAD, CAM, etc., in fact for all the requirements in the description. Because the suppliers came from specialist backgrounds in machine tools, design, computing and so on, the initiatives and successes were diverse. This telecommunications company has gone through this phase. It does not have a single computer embracing fully integrated activity, but a number of computers. They are interconnected as technical compatibility and opportunities have allowed. The company has the best examples of the CADMAT technology, but they are not from a single source.

Thirdly, comes the important step: to rationalize, to improve interconnections and to establish compatibility (Figure 5.3). This will eliminate the current duplication of some databases and further reduce the requirements for manual procedures and people. Theoretically, all those involved should learn about the issues of integration before committing themselves to the final links, but this has been impossible so far. The manufacturers of automatic machinery could not integrate with the CADMAT systems until CADMAT had been tried. CADMAT systems could not be designed and tested in integrated systems that did not yet exist. Large amounts of capital have been invested in this semi-integrated, piecewise-approach. As the capital is written off, the basis for future investment is at least clear.

Analysis

This company is a large one. Many thousands of man-hours have gone into professional analysis, business and technical, in order to decide what to do and when. Integration is here determined by push from technological progress and pull from the market which is aware of the latest ideas. The value of the case to the average manager is in illustrating hard integration, in introducing what is really a particular example of a flexible manufacturing system and in explaining more explicitly the term CADMAT.

Some opportunities and IT

The following examples illustrate the opportunistic use of IT to simplify operational activity. Methodology as such, is not discussed, but the reasons for change are clear.

Easing frustration and reducing financial slack

A small division of a high-technology company uses a computer for engineering and scientific work. It was frustrated by budgetary control from Head Office who regarded the difference between the year's budget and goods invoiced to date as spare money! The division, on the other hand, knew that a lot of long lead-time items were always outstanding and though not invoiced were nevertheless a commitment.

Of course, Head Office appreciated the argument but nevertheless they could not in practice keep their hands off the apparent surplus. The psychology was also bad in that they tended to reduce the following year's budget in line with the notional underspending! The division thus installed an accounting package on their own computer to handle their main purchasing. This includes commitment accounting and the division is able to send regular balance figures to Head Office. These seem to provide the legitimacy that Head Office requires.

More recently, a word processing package has also been added. Each secretary has a terminal, processor, disc drive and printer at a cost of about £2,000 a set which contrasts with £5,000 normally charged for dedicated word-processing units. A spare terminal has been provided for the engineers and scientists who can produce material themselves. For some technical work this is very efficient and in any case details can be tidied up by the secretaries as necessary.

Note the ubiquitous use of the computer without a central computer department. Note too the need for the divisional purchasing officer and his counterpart at Head Office to understand the role of the accounting package.

Difficulties can arise because responsibilities of secretaries, engineers and scientists are looser but in such companies, which are very task-oriented, the problems of status and of priorities are less troublesome than in more bureaucratic organizations where procedures and job descriptions are all important. Everyone likes the system most of the time. Management's role here is to make it work during the periods of breakdown and stress.

Tighter control and fewer debts

A company is a distributor of gravel and aggregates supplying materials from 20 sites spread over 100 miles. At each site a processing plant grades the materials which are supplied directly to customers. Each load is weighed and the sale acknowledged at the time of collection. The information is subsequently passed to Head Office and the customers are then invoiced. The nature of the business is determined by the building industry and the weather. Many sales are *ad hoc* and builders often have erratic cash flows and unsteady credit. To put a 'stop' on a customer who has become insolvent can take several days, and even then a site might fail to notice the fact and let a sale go through.

Computers and telecommunications have recently removed the problem as each site now records all its transactions on a small computer. Once a day these are transmitted to the Head Office computer which in turn updates their records of the status of all previous customers, putting stops on some and re-instating others. Future transactions for insolvent customers are thereby automatically blocked should they try to make a further purchase. The site operator does not have to perform near-impossible feats of memory and the computer link is only necessary for a few minutes each day. The combination of data processing and telecommunications is very effective.

Managing IT in smaller companies

The Head Office of a small conglomerate of companies in the East Midlands has a computer for finance and accounting purposes. There is an accountant who specializes in running the computer and an administration director with a special brief for IT technology. Within the basic corporate policy of the company it has been his job to stimulate interest in computer and data processing opportunities in the subsidiary companies. He has informal and regular contact with two local software houses and a nodding acquaintance with the main computer suppliers. He has much experience with maintenance contracts, and with software quality and implementation. His approach is to let any subsidiary decide what it wants for itself. He steps in to ensure that the software is intelligible and that if necessary they can find someone to deal with problems. The whole system must be reliably maintained and he would like them to bear in mind that at some future date their computers may need to communicate with the one at Head Office.

Each subsidiary now has a terminal and link to Head Office where all payroll and company accounts are processed centrally. Most subsidiaries have computers in operational areas of particular importance to themselves, ranging from cost accounting to production planning and control, plant monitoring and at a distribution company, semi-automatic recording of transactions.

Increased productivity and improved control

A large quarry in the North of England handles 600 lorries per day. During two intense periods of activity in early morning and afternoon, enormous amounts of manual paperwork used to be transacted each day which were then encoded and entered into a computer for invoicing and accounting purposes. An additional computer has since been installed at the weighbridge where the transactions initially occur. The resultant automation of the basic ordering and documentation has made little difference to the weighing procedures, although they are quicker and more disciplined. However, the basic data may now be passed automatically to the accounting computer. It is fuller than the accounting data and contains information about the market, where the loads go, what materials are used by which customers, whether the patterns of supply are changing, which materials are most popular, and so on. The company has thus dispensed with the services of two accounts clerks, the sales manager, his car and expense account. The truth is that the general manager can do the necessary supervision of the weighbridge operation because the computer has reduced the management problem to one simply of maintaining procedure. There is no longer any preoccupation with chasing sales figures because these are contained in reliable and regular computer reports. The sales and managing directors can handle the other functions of the former sales manager and are better informed as a result.

A catastrophic influence

One steel company which installed a computer to monitor order progress through the works, was suddenly faced with a problem. When the sales department began to receive computer reports of load on capacity, above anything ever previously obtained, it became very clear that the policy on delivery promises was suspect. In truth, there was no policy but the issue was now exposed by the computer. It was necessary to decide whether (i) to continue in an *ad hoc* way (policy = no policy) or (ii) to set delivery promises according to a pre-determined program of rolling at the mill (sell free capacity), or (iii) to roll orders according to date of receipt and a notion of customer priority (sell steel and hopefully a service).

The company was recently wound up, not because of the installation of the computer but in part due to the weak corporate policy that the computer revealed and the subsequent management turmoil that ensued.

Smooth operations and rough markets

This case concerns one cigarette company but is probably representative of all major cigarette companies. With the exception of a few developing countries, the market for cigarettes is slowly declining because of the circumstantial connections with cancer, heart disease and general ill health. Competition between suppliers is thus severe. Brands of different quality and blend distinguish the 'products' and customers choose their 'brand' partly on price, partly for subjective reasons and partly out of loyalty. Advertising and marketing campaigns are thus critically important but have to be backed by efficient production to keep within the range of prices set by the market, to stand any chance at all.

The company currently has twenty brands in order to compete across the range. This is a relatively small number, but the manufacturing plant has to respond to the demands created by various marketing campaigns throughout the world. Many of these are in response to competitors' efforts and thus relatively uncontrolled. From a production point of view the demand is market driven and appears as if it were customer oriented.

The manufacturing activity is shown schematically in Figure 5.4. Primary production commences with the procurement of different types of leaf and stem tobacco. These are held as raw material stock in ten silos from whence they are drawn as required for cutting, drying and blending. The

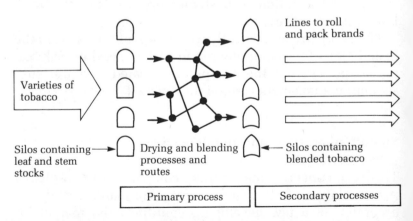

Figure 5.4 Cigarette manufacturing processes

actual processes require careful control. Different processes and process routes are used for different blends which are stored in a second set of ten silos.

Secondary production consists of some twelve production lines which may be set up to make any particular brand; rolling cigarettes and packing them into both hand packs and distribution cartons. The setting up of a line requires a lot of attention to detail such as the blend, packaging, paper, length, tip and promotion vouchers, which as shown in Figure 5.5 are all brand dependent.

If the silos have insufficient blended tobacco to meet a required production run there is a problem in rescheduling the primary processes to meet the demand. A silo of blended tobacco that remains unused for a long time reduces the flexibility of the system and incurs heavy costs since the duty paid on it is very high. Operationally there is a soft integration problem in economically linking market requirements and production. The problem of being effective in the

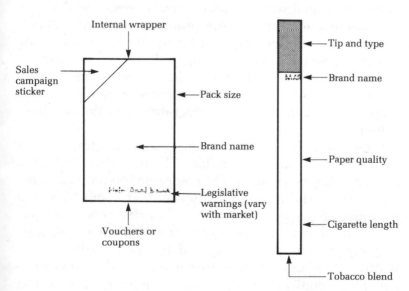

Figure 5.5 Cigarette product, specification details

market and efficient at using resources arises once again. Slack is represented by the unnecessary quantities of silo tobacco or in not being able to meet a retail demand for a given brand.

Hard integration is evident in the automatic control of the primary processes. A central control room with impressive instrumentation allows a shift engineer to run most of this operation single-handed. There are alarms and fault detectors which provide him with sufficient information to despatch a maintenance technician to rectify any technical problems. Most of the secondary, cigarette-making machines are also instrumented and provide fault, production and wastage figures to a central display and data-logging unit. This system also identifies each machine with its operator. (Unduly high wastage may mean lack of operator skill and a need for retraining.)

The company also has a central computer for sales, purchasing, financial planning, payroll and costing purposes. It is not integrated with the secondary process and does not have automatic access to the production records. This is because the computers monitoring the machinery are 'process oriented' and not compatible with the 'business-system oriented' mainframe at Head Office. The primary process, computer control is not connected to either of the other systems so complete integration has not yet been achieved.

Integration is probably progressing as fast as the company can safely assimilate IT, in either technical, human or financial terms. The co-ordination problem is not a matter for IT but one for intellect and inspiration. The operations have been reduced to a flow-line as far as is practical and the man-management issues have been considerably reduced by the widespread use of machinery. It is worth noting, nevertheless, that maintenance and trouble-shooting technicians have replaced the manual worker as the principal subject of labour relations.

External integration is not particularly well addressed by IT, although the computer is used for monitoring sales trends and in support of financial and forecasting programs (models).

6 Integration, responsibilities, control and implementation

Introduction

This chapter is concerned with the detailed implementation of IT. The examples (Chapter 5) and methodology (Chapter 4) indicate the opportunities for IT and means of assessing them in different forms of organization and sectors of industry. It is already clear from Chapter 4, that to achieve integration it is necessary to clarify responsibilities and to reconcile functional responsibilities of different activities with a wider responsibility to organizational strategic objectives. Otherwise, integration would essentially have been achieved as an end in itself with effects possibly detrimental to the organization's survival.

Table 4.3 summarizes the three principial emphases that corporate responsibilities might have, which could provide the basis for a practical definition of corporate aims when none other are available. It is clearly necessary to balance the responsibilities of profit/loss, efficiency and effectiveness over a period of time because there are practical difficulties in pursuing more than one objective at a time.

The design and implementation of IT should aim to ensure that pertinent information is provided to those in the organization who bear responsibility. Integration may be said to be successful when those who bear responsibility are enabled to fulfil their responsibilities. Moreover, those responsibilities are fulfilled in a predictable manner through particular actions. Successful integration, therefore, means that the organization is a controlled system with each of its sub-systems relating to each other in a compatible way. The implementation phase requires detailed awareness of what each sub-system needs in order to achieve control. Before dealing in detail with the stages involved in the implementation of IT, it is necessary to outline what control involves.

Control system principles

There are four elements in a controlled system, and all managers use them, unknowingly in most cases. They are:

1. Awareness of purpose, usually expressed as an AIM.
2. Ability to formulate a PLAN or strategy to achieve the aim. This involves information, IT or paperwork and infers some reasoning or reconciliation of factors (including feedback).
3. ACTION to carry out the plan, physical activity in many cases.
4. FEEDBACK which involves the monitoring of the outcome of the action in units of measure appropriate to the original plan.

The proposition here is to take control, with its four elements as the basic means for achieving integration. The smallest sub-unit is the individual, either as himself or, where appropriate, as a manager. These individuals go together towards making the company itself. We can extend Argenti's control model of the manager (Figure 6.1) to the individual (Figure 6.2) by including the influence of personal goals in addition to those of the company. In Figure 6.2 the individual, in planning how to carry out a task will, implicitly or explicitly, take into account such matters as his chance of being able to do the task (skills), the likelihood that performing the task will meet his personal goals (wage payments, job satisfaction and other aims), and the aims of the company. These factors together, which are essentially the expectations approach (see Chapter 3), should determine the level of the individual's motivation to perform the

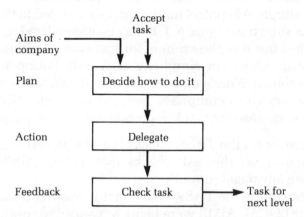

Figure 6.1 Control model of a manager

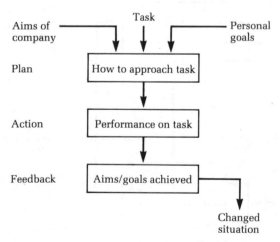

Figure 6.2 Control model of an individual

task and the level at which he performs (his action). The checking of his performance against his aims provides the individual with feedback to adjust his plan where necessary.

The simplified control model can be extended to the company as shown in Figure 6.3. It may be generalized for many activities, but it is shown here for just two activities, *sales* and *production*. For simplicity also, only the operational level is shown. Notice that control of both the sales and production activities comprises the four elements. Note also that in each case feedback is present for several purposes:

1. Whoever set the TASK checks that it was performed.
2. Whoever set the task checks that THEIR AIMS were being advanced (or not).
3. Those doing the TASK check that it was performed and their LOCAL AIMS were being advanced (or not).

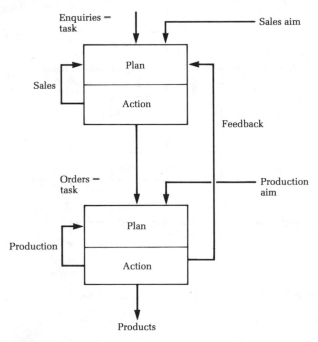

Figure 6.3 Example of company model

The distinction between an AIM and a TASK is important, particularly in relation to human goals. In a company the aim may be to achieve sales revenue of £1,000,000. This is not the same as the task of selling. A cabinet maker may have the task of making furniture which is not the same as the aim of being a master craftsman.

The concept of control infers that aims are not likely to be achieved automatically—various factors have to be manipulated. In any company, management control involves the co-ordination of various tasks. The way in which this is done and the degree of success achieved will be influenced by such things as, variations and disturbances in the environment around the individual and the company, the size, ownership and technology of the company and the behaviour of individuals. The contingencies of environment, size, ownership and technology will affect the way in which the control is organized within the company. The behaviour of individuals will be influenced by the way in which their own goals agree or conflict with those of the company and in turn affect their expectations. The control system will be constrained to the extent that control cannot be exercised over an environment which demands action beyond the limits of the system and to the extent that the skills and motivation of individuals constrain their ability to plan and act.

The criticisms of automatic control-type models are that systems which include people are too highly adaptive and their aims too difficult to discern. This is really an admission that we are unable to quantify critically important parameters rather than a criticism of the model. In the absence of these parameters any approach is, of course, limited, but the use of responsibility as a means of assessing aims is always valid.

For example, a company, its managers and its employees are also part of the population at large. There are two systems of direct interest, the 'company' and the wider 'system of people'. They coexist, with the latter having indeterminate boundaries because the non-employees in the population influence the employees. The systems, almost by definition, are in a dynamic state of balance whereby all the individuals are striving to achieve or have achieved their aims (public, company and personal), through their plans, their actions and their responsibilities to the plans and actions of others (company and public). They do this within the current ambience of attitudes, constraints on resources and limitations of skill. Why a company is performing as it does can be explained. However, the 'problem' is more usually posed as: 'Why is it *not performing* in some other way?' Again the theory helps us. To perform in a particular way involves prerequisites, the determination of which spring directly from the model and form the basis for the detailed methodology in the next section.

Methodology

This second part of the overall methodology discussed in Chapter 4 is directed towards the system designer or innovator. It is assumed that a preliminary study has been carried out and that those involved are familiar with the existing activities and organization. The steps are thence as follows:

Step 1

Why is innovation being considered? Is this to satisfy some personal goal of the person suggesting it, is it to satisfy some identifiable aim for the company, or is it a mixture of the two? If it is largely for the individual, there may be doubts about the amount of motivation that can be raised in the rest of the company in support of the intended change.

Step 2

Is the suggested innovation relevant and valid? Is there some better, other innovation or change which is relevant and valid? Is it compatible with the aims (company and personal) of those responsible for agreeing to it? If not, it is futile to proceed.

The second step is a demanding one and requires analysis and the exercise of judgement. Proceed as follows:

(i)   What are the principal subdivisions of responsibility in the company, e.g. sites, divisions, sections, departments, functions?

(ii) Are these subdivisions consistent with the subdivision of functions, e.g. do Sales staff actually have authority over selling?

(iii) Are the sub-areas of responsibility (activity) controllable, e.g. are they of such a size that they can be led towards a specific objective? The factors affecting this are the numbers of people involved, the quality of leadership, and the incentive to pursue company aims, particularly in relation to their compatibility with personal goals and company aims. If the sub-areas are not controllable, then further subdivisions of activity, changes of leadership, modifications to incentives etc. must be considered.

(iv) Are the aims of a given sub-area consistent with the company's overall aim and with the aims of other sub-areas? Are the aims specified in terms which are of practical use in planning that activity and utilizing feedback? For example the aims, 'do your best' and 'increase output' are perhaps worthy, but inadequate. They have unknown implications for other sub-areas (particularly at operational level) and weaken their plans and actions.

(v)   Does the control information receive support from the management information system? Do policies exist in relation to operations and the allocation of resources? The one affects the external performance to customers and from suppliers, the other affects internal performance. To be supportive some quantifying of policy should be evident in the information system. Examples might be recommended levels of stocks and work-in-progress, lead times, mix and manning. The units of measure and different representations cited in Chapter 4, Figure 4.2 are very relevant.

(vi) Do procedures exist at the operational level to ensure that control information has (reasonable) integrity?

(vii) Do the senior managers recognize their responsibilities towards the control system, e.g. towards the other sub-areas of responsibility and do they appreciate that there is a company aim as well as sub-area aims and personal goals?

Upon reaching question (vii) one should have a clear idea of the fundamental issues, of why the company is performing as it does and whether it can be controlled to achieve any other kind of objective. The steps are consistent with the control concept:

1. Start with the AIM
2. Proceed to PLAN
3. Then carry out ACTIONS
4. Is the aim being advanced FEEDBACK

Unfortunately the why is not usually answerable from direct observation. It is the ACTION (or what), as indicated in the physical activity, and the PLAN (or how) as expressed in the details of the organization and procedures, which are prominent in reality and thus most easily examined. Their investigation is also a significant portion of any analysis and innovation must eventually cause changes at this level. Their priority is, however, not as fundamental as that of resolving and reconciling aims. The following practical technique for examining a company epitomizes this distinction.

Step 3

(i) Examine the organization from the top, following the delegation of authority (responsibility) as defined by the previous higher level and test each sub-area as expressed in Step 2 ((i)–(vii)). This is an AIM (responsibility)-oriented, fundamental approach.

(ii) Examine the tasks which the company performs at the operational level; market forecast through sales to production, invoicing and despatch, for example. What evidence is there, looking 'upwards' into the organization, that actions are influenced by plans and a recognition of company aims? What evidence is there that sub-areas are pulling towards a coherent set of aims? This is an *activity-oriented* pragmatic approach, which is necessary but inclined to lose impetus in the mass of detail, the purpose of which may not be properly perceived because it relates to large numbers of people and includes their attempts to achieve personal goals as well as their contributions to company activity.

In practice either method may be used to illicit information and a combination is very often a workable compromise.

(Stages of proposal, discussion, specification, design, test and implementation would normally follow. These stages raise issues about good practice but, in this context, few points of principle. They are omitted to avoid obscuring the fundamentals.)

Example case

This case concerns the real company shown schematically in Figure 6.4. Metal is melted at a Central Facility and distributed to two casting plants, A and B, at a distance of 3 kilometres. It is transported in large ladles on bogeys, pulled by general purpose locomotives. At the Central Facility scrap metal is melted in a furnace, mixed with additives in a special ladle and then transferred to the transport ladles by crane. The time taken to provide a ladle from

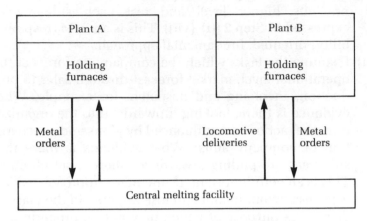

Figure 6.4 Co-ordination of metal movement

receipt of a request is approximately one hour provided there is a regular demand on the furnace. The locomotives take the ladles to the casting plants where metal is poured into electric holding furnaces. From these the metal is drawn for casting as required. Each transport ladle contains twice the capacity of the holding furnaces and stands until both the 'first' and 'second' pours have emptied it.

The problem was that the casting plants were running out of metal thereby causing several hundred men and expensive plant to stand idle. This was quite aside from time lost due to technical faults and disputes. The reasons were thought to be in 'the running of the Central Facility and Casting Plants'. A number of consultants had investigated the situation and there were broadly two kinds of suggested solution. One concentrated on gathering information about everything and the development of an algorithm for instructing those involved about what actions to follow all the time. The other type left the decisions of what to do with those involved and concentrated on clarifying their aims. Proposals of the first type were rejected. A proposal of the second type was accepted and implemented because, among other reasons they considered that 'it helped them to do their job'. The innovations followed the methodology already discussed, with the following answers to the questions posed being obtained:

Step 1. There was a clear reason for innovation, namely to reduce stoppages due to poor co-ordination.

Step 2. It was valid: the managers agreed the reason and there was clear evidence for the stoppages in works records.

(i). The subdivisions were: Central Melting Facility, Casting Plants A and B, Holding Furnaces A and B, and Locomotives.

(ii). Responsibility for the locomotives was transferred from the transport manager to the Central Melting Facility Manager, to make activity consistent with responsibilities.

(iii). The size and organization of each subdivision did not appear to pose problems. Morale and leadership were good. Aims were unclear and ill-conditioned and the Melting Facility Foreman's expectations of the Casting Plants were that orders and times were suspect and to be treated with caution. There were always at least two versions of 'recent history'. The principal redefinitions of aims were:

The Central Melting Facility Foreman was given responsibility for meeting orders for metal to supply Holding Furnaces A and B, on time. Previously, his responsibility for ensuring they did not run out of metal was unrealistic because there were too many factors outside his knowledge and beyond his control. The aim was to minimize the error between actual time of delivery and ordered time.

The Holding Furnace Supervisors were made responsible for the content of their furnaces unless the Melting Plant should fail to deliver. They were made responsible for ordering metal at least 60 minutes in advance of the delivery time. This caused them to improve their local communications with the Casting Shop Foremen, particularly about casting rates. Their aim was to have metal available for casting within the constraint of a 60-minute lead time on supply.

The Locomotive Foreman was made responsible for getting full ladles to the plants on time and retrieving ladles

as soon as they were emptied. This is the Locomotive Foreman's proper function, but it had been in another area of
responsibility for historical reasons which were no longer
applicable.

(iv). The aims were already consistent. Sales and the
Producing Plants had compatible aims. Their plans, action
and feedback elements were in good order. It was possible
to avoid involving other sub-areas in the resolution of the
problem.

(v) and (vi). Procedures at the Central Melting Facility
and at the Holding Furnaces were modified. The main
features were the introduction of a common clock which
automatically timed orders and a display to indicate the
status of current orders to the Plants and Melting Facility.
The common clock provides the basis for reliable feedback.

(vii). The managers were careful to note the definitions
of responsibility. The accounting system is able to assign
the cost of stoppages more exactly to the Casting Plants or
the Melting Facility by virtue of the common clock. Lateness of an order (Holding Furnace error) or lateness of
delivery (Melting Facility error) are distinguishable and the
new system is thus fairer as well as more effective. The
extent of tangible benefits is a matter for analysis and being
in the early stages of implementation the cost effectiveness
has yet to be determined.

Conclusions

This case has emphasized the usual concern with the *what*
and *how* of a system. It emphasizes the importance of
asking *why* a change is being made and that systems are a
natural product of their constituent parts. There may be no
such thing as a 'bad' system, merely systems which have
incompatible or 'wrong' objectives. Without some real
effort to define corporate objectives—by the senior
managers, for example—a company will adopt a dynamic

equilibrium which simply reflects the attempts of all its members to achieve their personal aims and goals. The definition of corporate objectives is, however, often difficult and unclear. This chapter shows how the careful consideration of responsibilities can provide the aim or purpose which is so important for any control system, management control systems in particular, to work.

References

J. Argenti, *A Management System for the Seventies*, Allen and Unwin, 1972.

T. Burns and G. M. Stalker, *Management of Innovation*, Tavistock, 1965.

J. L. Machin, 'A Contingent Methodology for Management Control', *Journal of Management Studies*, pp. 1–29, February 1979.

D. J. Rhodes, D. M. Wright and M. G. Jarrett, *Computers, Information and Manufacturing Systems*, Holt-Saunders, (1984).

D. J. Rhodes, D. M. Wright and M. G. Jarrett, 'Simple Diagnostic Tool for Improving Control of Manufacturing Systems', *Proceedings of the Instituion of Electrical Engineers*, Part A, June 1982.

D. J. Rhodes and D. M. Wright, 'Coordination of Metal Movements at a Pipe-Spinning Plant: Concepts and the Computerised System', *J. Engineering Costs and Production Economics*, April 1985.

J. Woodward, *Industrial Organisation: Behaviour and Control*, Oxford University Press, 1970.

D. M. Wright, D. J. Rhodes and M. G. Jarrett, 'Management Control for Effective Corporate Planning', *Long Range Planning*, August 1984.

7 Managing the introduction of IT in a not-for-profit service organization*

Introduction

The case study material presented in the previous two chapters has referred solely to commercial organizations. This chapter deals with the not-for-profit non-commercial service organization, and uses the case of the British National Health Service (NHS) to illustrate the problems involved in managing the introduction of IT. This type of organization can raise different issues than 'for-profit' organizations, because of the nature of the organization and the nature of change involving the introduction of IT. In particular, in the NHS, the problems arising from the influence of parliamentary and government department control, a bureaucratic system which produces resistance to change, and the very considerable influence of the medical and nursing professions which can draw upon public sympathy to help emasculate proposals for change, have to be dealt with. Moreover, the operation of the NHS takes place within the context of an organizational objective of adequate public provision of medical care for all which often outweighs financial and efficiency constraints. However, such a context can bring into sharp focus many of the broader issues concerning the introduction of change and of IT in particular which were discussed in Chapters 2 and 3. These issues concern the following:

● implementing IT in the presence or absence of rapid environmental change (environmental jolts/crisis);

* A shortened version of this chapter appears in *International Journal of Operations and Production Management*, 1985, vol. 5, no. 3.

- the difficulty of implementing IT where the management hierarchy, though bureaucratic in some senses, does not possess line authority;
- the problem of implementing IT which involves the integration of functions in the absence of line authority and in the presence of management by consensus;
- the role of an external agent for change, who is both able to push through change and collaborate with those performing the functions to be computerized, where internal skills are absent;
- the difficulties involved in converting a formulated IT strategy into a practical reality.

The chapter starts by outlining the overall general management structure in the British NHS, drawing attention to its ability to deal with change and with the attempts which have been made to strengthen this ability. The second section briefly discusses recent approaches to the introduction of IT in the NHS. Both these two sections serve as background to the third which discusses the case of the introduction of computerized work scheduling in one large hospital where the shock to change was brought about through public concern over the quality of patient care.

The British National Health Service—organizational structure and changes

The major structural change in the NHS was introduced in 1974 and was concerned with strengthening control in four main ways: through the unification of administration for health services; through changes in the relationship between central and local administration; through a clarification of managerial roles and relationships, based on industrial management experience and principles; and, something which tended to counteract the last named, the co-option of professional groups into management. This reorganization was designed to produce clearer lines of organizational accountability and to strengthen the control of the centre, and may be depicted as in Figure 7.1. It is important to notice that at each of the Regional, Area and District levels in the organization there were to be management teams which were comprised of representatives of the administrative, nursing and medical functions. The job of these teams was to manage by consensus. The 1982 reorganization of the NHS was intended to slim the bureaucratic structure by removing the Area level between Region and District (Figure 7.2), and by delegating more power to the unit level, below the district. However, consensus management teams still remained an essential feature of the organization.

Consensus management has been subject to a great deal of criticism; the main grounds are usually that: consensus management reduces to dealing with trivial items, weakens accountability, slows decision-making, places teams under considerable pressure to achieve consensus, produces weak decisions, leads to agendas which concentrate on incremental rather than contentious issues and is likely to be dominated by strong personalities. Whilst recognizing that there is some validity in these criticisms, Harrison has pointed out the importance of this type of approach given the different sub-objectives of the interested parties who comprise the consensus management teams. Members of the teams are often in competition for scarce resources and may not share the organization's objective. Hence, although the structure of the NHS may be based on the notion that all share the same objective (a unitary view) the behaviour of the constituent power groups may undermine the strength of this argument. A pluralist viewpoint is, therefore, perhaps a more accurate description of reality.

The methodology outlined in Chapter 4 indicates that the above arrangement is both unsatisfactory for achieving adequate control of the organization and, of great importance here, inadequate for effecting change. The problems

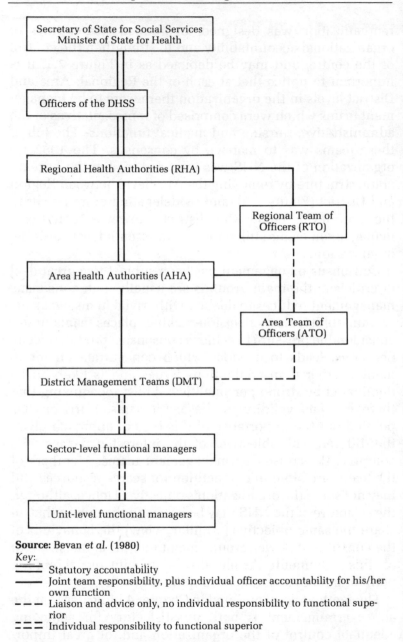

Source: Bevan *et al.* (1980)

Key:

═══ Statutory accountability

───── Joint team responsibility, plus individual officer accountability for his/her own function

─ ─ ─ Liaison and advice only, no individual responsibility to functional superior

═ ═ ═ Individual responsibility to functional superior

Figure 7.1 NHS organizational structure 1974 to 1982

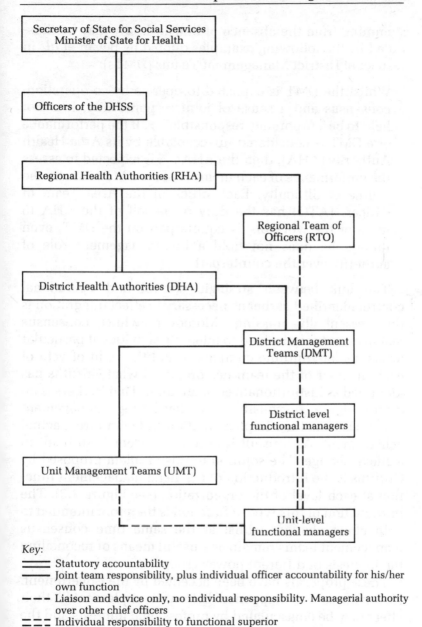

Key:
══════ Statutory accountability
────── Joint team responsibility, plus individual officer accountability for his/her
       own function
─ ─ ─ Liaison and advice only, no individual responsibility. Managerial authority
       over other chief officers
═ ═ ═ Individual responsibility to functional superior

Figure 7.2 NHS organizational structure post 1982

stemming from the absence of line authority may be illustrated by the following examples quoted by Bevan *et al.* in
respect of District Management Teams (DMTs):

> Whilst the DMT is expected to operate by co-operation,
> consensus and a sense of joint responsibility, it is not
> held to be 'corporately responsible' . . . If the performance
> of a DMT is considered unacceptable by its Area Health
> Authority (AHA), then the AHA . . . is expected to assess
> the performance of each member of the DMT to assess the
> source of difficulty. Each office of the Area Team of
> Officers (ATO) has the duty on behalf of the AHA to
> monitor the work of his counterpart on the DMT, even
> though he does not hold a line-management role of
> authority over the counterpart.

The link between strategic control and operational
control identified earlier as necessary to effect integration is
thus essentially missing. Moreover, whilst consensus
management may be held to integrate activities at particular
levels, its labyrinthine complexity and the right of veto of
each member of the team has produced what Griffiths has
identified as institutionalized stagnation. That is, there is no
driving force responsible for developing management
plans, securing their implementation and monitoring actual
achievement. As a result it becomes extremely difficult to
achieve change. The solution to this problem proposed by
Griffiths is the introduction of a general management function at each level of the organization (see Figure 7.3). The
introduction of this type of function is therefore intended to
help effect change, whilst at the same time consensus
management teams remain as a useful means of reconciling
the interests of different power groups.

These proposals have been accepted by the Government.
However, as has happened before, if implemented their
effect may be emasculated by professional interests and the
influence of the Department of Health and Social Security
in day-to-day matters could remain incompatibly strong.

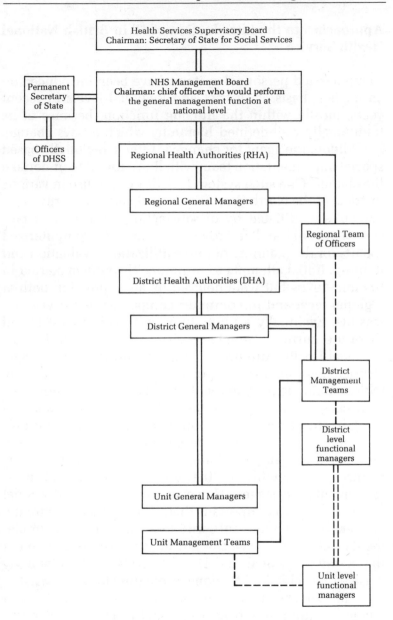

Figure 7.3 Proposed form of organizational structure following Griffiths (1983)

Approaches to the introduction of IT in British National Health Service

Computerized personnel systems have been introduced on an *ad hoc* basis at District and Regional levels in recent years, mostly within the nursing function, because of its traditionally well-defined hierarchy which allows change. In addition, the agent for change is often a regionally based special implementation team with line support to undertake the change. One such system is SNIPPET, in use in various districts of the North West Regional Health Authority. This system was initiated by dissatisfaction with manual personnel records and it provides a range of computerized reports for the planning of nurse utilization, evaluation and training. Initial attempts to introduce the system started in the mid-1970s but were delayed by an impression both at regional level and in computer companies that it was not feasible. Eventually a pilot study was made in 1981, and there are currently nineteen Districts in the North West Regional Health Authority using the Information Package. District Co-ordinators, responsible to the District Nursing Officer, train the users and hold regular meetings with users to discuss enhancements to the system. Users are trained on the job, after attending a computer appreciation (not programming!) course prior to implementation. Collaboration between the agent for change and the system user thus features very highly at the implementation and post-implementation stages. However, from an organizational point of view it is important that, though District Nursing Officers have the line authority to ensure that IT is implemented, they also have the power to refuse to implement the system. Regional and District levels in the hierarchy liaise with each other, Region cannot direct District what to do. The pattern of implementation across the NHS as a whole has until now been very patchy. To some extent it represents the earlier stages described in Chapter 4, where enthusiasts or 'entrepreneurs' try to take the initiative.

The Körner Report into manpower planning in the NHS recommended the introduction of an integrated system across the nursing, medical and administrative functions. This system is intended to provide for the routine collection of the relevant information required to run the NHS effectively, paying particular attention to the control and efficient use of manpower, annual and strategic planning and policy development, the determination of terms and conditions of service, and accountability. The Report explicitly recognizes the importance of an integrated information system, which draws together manpower, activity and financial data, in the efficient and effective use of staff. The base point of data collection is to be the District level.

In this way, an IT-based manpower planning strategy is proposed. However, the move from proposal to practical reality may not be easy. The implementation of the Griffiths proposals, which would introduce some element of line authority may promote such far-reaching changes. But, the recruitment of general managers to fill these line posts has been difficult, particularly given the well-known ability of professional interests to frustrate change. The retention of the consensus management element in the NHS organization makes it doubtful whether the use of IT in one function can be extended across functions within a reasonable timescale, if at all. Even with teams experienced in the introduction of IT as the agents of change and with collaborative efforts, IT may be rendered ineffective or its emphasis changed from that intended by Körner. In an organization insulated from its environment, as the NHS has been until now, such a result seems more than likely. Threats to privatize parts of the NHS are unlikely to strengthen the desire to effect changes. But the professional elements in the NHS are sensitive to factors which call into question the quality of patient care. Thus the prospects for successful change, with minimal delay and resistance, in an organization such as the NHS where line management is weak, are likely to be best under some kind of 'crisis' conditions.

The following NHS case study illustrates the importance of 'crisis' in the successful implementation of a computerized control system and in producing the atmosphere conducive to acceptance of change, which the leader was able to build upon. Collaboration from employees and the support of senior management were also important in achieving success.

The introduction of computerized information technology for scheduling nurses' duties in the NHS may be particularly suited for initiating collaborative work. The IT application concerns real activity at the point where the organization 'does its job' and cares for patients. It is a point at which achievements occur and where they can be influenced. Collaboration is required both to assimilate improved information and to reduce resistance to change. Such resistance may arise from fears of loss of power and from antipathy towards those wishing to effect change who are perceived as uncommitted to the priority of adequate patient care at any price. The role of leader may be especially important where adequate skills are absent, a rigorous time-scale needs to be adhered to, and where the system of consensus management makes it difficult for any one of the constituent members of the team to take a lead.

The introduction of a computerized system for scheduling nursing duties, which illustrates this approach in practice is discussed in the next section.

Case study—high-security mental hospital

Background

The case concerns a high-security mental hospital. A great deal of resources is devoted to the nursing function, far in excess of that encountered in a general hospital. In order that wards are staffed fully to strict requirements within the constraint of finite resources, nursing allocation assumes a high level of importance.

The Nurse Allocation function is concerned with the day-to-day and short-term allocation of nurses to wards and duties within a generally agreed framework of shift working and leave, covering a six-week cycle. The prime responsibility of the nursing officers carrying out this task is to maintain the appropriate manning levels and mix of grades. It covers approximately 700 nurses in four divisions totalling over fifty wards and operating 24 hours per day for 365 days per year. The officers in charge are expected to exercise judgement in:

- selecting nurses to make up compatible teams for wards and duties;
- maintaining manning levels despite sickness, leaves, attendance on courses, and outside escorts;
- assigning extra duties and overtime equitably (economy is not a prime concern).

Judgement is needed for the preparation of the daily lists of all nursing duties, in the preparation of the six-week schedules and for the telephone calls, re-adjustments and trouble-shooting that characterize office activity. There are also strict requirements and a responsibility for monitoring attendance and keeping records. The overall task of allocations is manifest in a daily routine which normally involves a considerable amount of list writing and re-writing.

Prior to the introduction of the computerized system, discussed below, the organizational context in which the nursing allocation officers carried out their tasks was as follows. As may be seen from Figure 7.4 the nursing allocation officers, as with other nursing officers were responsible to five Senior Nursing Officers (the SNO-Admin. was introduced after the installation of the computer). For each six-week cycle each SNO would assess the staff who normally worked under his supervision, their leave and training requirements, and the staffing needs of their division. This information was passed to the nursing allocation officers so

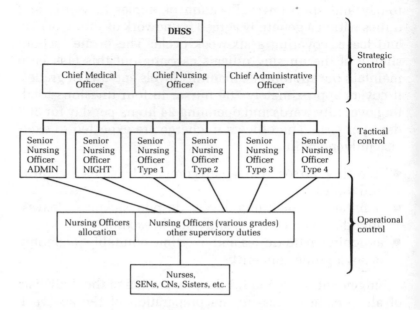

Figure 7.4 Hospital organizational structure

that they could prepare detailed schedules of staffing for the four divisions. (The remaining SNO covered all four day-time divisions at night.)

Complications arose in practice for two main reasons. First, each SNO had his own system of staffing, particularly as related to overtime allocation which played an important part in supplementing the income of staff. This fragmented approach complicated the work of the nursing allocation officers. Second, the line of accountability of the nursing allocation officers was not very clear. Although in practice they were responsible to the SNO in the largest division, they were effectively accountable to all SNOs. The result of these two problems was what in management terms may be referred to as a power game. That is, the two nursing alloca-tion officers could make trade-offs between the SNOs and the SNOs would attempt to influence the way in which nurses were allocated so as to help the management of their own divisions.

A system such as this, though reconciling the needs of each function in a sub-optimal way, was acceptable in practice for a number of years. As long as wards were staffed according to the regulations, then the Chief Nursing Officer was under little pressure to become involved in remedying such imperfections. Miller has shown how a system can absorb imperfections in the absence of crisis conditions and, in the NHS generally line management as found in a private sector manufacturing organization is rather weak. When periods of severe environmental stress do arise a management control system must be at least re-examined, if not replaced.

For the Hospital, such conditions arose in the late 1970s and early 1980s when a series of allegations of ill-treatment of patients led to legal proceedings against a number of nurses and their subsequent imprisonment and/or dismissal. This episode initiated an enquiry into the running of the hospital and, in particular, into the way in which nurses were allocated to wards, in an attempt to prevent such problems arising again.

This enquiry identified the possible need for a computer-based system of nurse allocation. There was no skill available in-house which could implement such a system, nor were there adequate links with other parts of the NHS or DHSS which could provide the necessary skills. An approach was thus made to a consultant (one of the authors) in specially adapted control systems. The outside consultant was independent and able to work to short deadlines without the bureaucratic procedures which are a significant feature of the NHS.

Implementation

The implementation followed the multi-staged approach outlined in Chapter 4 and from the initial proposal to the posting of the first six-week schedule took approximately 9 months, with the phased introduction of the computer, programs and training in the last 4 months.

At each stage of implementation several visits were made to the hospital to provide training and to help sort out the procedures needed to run the computer smoothly alongside the other activities in the Allocations Office. The daily patterns of work are completely altered by the computer since the emphasis has changed from writing lists to following computer procedure. The four Senior Nursing Officers of the four Divisions have had to form a consensus view towards the innovation and to adjust their procedures for notifying changes to Allocations. The relationship between Nursing and Administration has been affected by the changes to clerical work, to the form of communication of overtime to the wages section and to recording courses.

Features of the system

Although the principal purpose of the system was to improve the allocation of nurses there were in fact a group of functions which had to be treated either together or not at all. The principal features are as follows.

(a) Monitoring establishment strength

This records the nominal and actual manning levels by ward and division, by numbers and grade of nurse as shown in Table 7.1. Changes in the levels are incorporated as simple amendments. The program can thus present the nominal and actual hours available for comparison with the hours actually worked, as reported from the records of nurse allocations. It can retain a record of the variations in establishment strength over a given period of time.

(b) Staff lists and course records

The details in the six-week schedules, the day sheets and the overtime records, which are discussed below, depend

Table 7.1 Establishment records, 10 September 1984

Grade	Nurses F.T.	Part time Nurses	Hours	Equiv. F.T.	Total
Area 2 staff in post					
DIV					
SNO					
NO					
C/N	46	1	36.00	0.96	46.96
SN	12	36	783.00	20.88	32.88
ENS	36	11	300.00	8.00	44.00
NA	75	83	1700.00	45.33	120.33
OTH	—	—	—	—	—
Total	169	131	2819.00	75.17	244.17
Total staff in post					
DIV	1	—	—	—	1.00
SNO	4	—	—	—	4.00
NO	17	—	—	—	17.00
C/N	119	2	72.00	1.92	120.92
SN	41	68	1529.00	40.77	81.77
ENS	128	72	1735.00	46.26	174.26
NA	225	195	4211.00	112.28	337.26
OTH	—	—	—	—	—
Total	535	337	7547.00	201.23	736.21

upon the computer having a full list of all staff with information about them which might affect the drawing up of these documents, such as:

- What shift pattern does this nurse work?
- What leave dates apply?
- Is he/she on a course during the scheduled period?

Once the computer list had been compiled it could easily be amended to account for changes in ward, leave and shift patterns. Provided they are entered, the effects of courses, ward changes, and so on all appear automatically in the next six-week schedule.

The inclusion of course attendance means that a list of all courses which involve absence from duty is held in the computer and each new course must be entered to keep it up to date. Any nurse booked to attend a course is assigned to it and the computer can then include this information in the schedules. Since 'records' are the responsibility of the Personnel Department, this information and the demarcation of responsibility are a potential issue. In this case the attendance on 'fire' and other such courses by all nurses within a twelve-month period, meant that the planned release of nurses from wards and duties was largely initiated from the Nursing Divisions and Allocations Office. Personnel are always informed so as to keep their comprehensive records up to date but the 'who hasn't been on a fire course yet?' type of question can better be answered by the computer than by someone searching a file. Personnel continue with the main records; the small subset in Allocations is not in conflict with them.

(c) *Six-week schedules*
Six-week schedules are posted every six weeks to inform all nurses of their work patterns. The computer contains an (electronic) copy of the printed list, shown in Table 7.2, which can be amended to conform with changes in circumstance as they arise, for example, sickness, special leave changes to middle days, etc. The impact of the computer here was to cause a re-clarification of what the leave keys and shift patterns really meant so that they could be used properly in the computer. Table 7.3 illustrates typical shift patterns, where a day is to be worked unless otherwise indicated, and leave keys. These items are stored as written and are exactly as formerly used before the computer. This was important to ensure that the different combinations of leave dates and shift patterns were applied consistently and did not 'rob anyone of a middle day', for example. It is possible to rotate the shift patterns automatically each six weeks. The annual leaves can also be rotated without altering the

Table 7.2 Part of a six-week schedule

09/10/83   SIX WEEK SCHEDULE MENTAL ILLNESS DIVISION

COMMENCING 9 OCTOBER

		S	WARD	SH	9	10	11	12	13	14	15	16	17	18	19	20	ETC.
					S	M	T	W	T	F	S	S	M	T	W	T	
CN	HILL C	M	GREY	A	C	C	C	C	C	C	C	C	C	C	C	C	
SN	ALLEN S	M	GREY	A	O		O			O	O	O		O	L	O	
SN	WILLIAMS AP	M	GREY	A	L	O	L	O	L	O	L	O	L	O	M	O	
SN	FARRELL P	M	GREY	A	O			O			O	O	O	O		O	ETC.
SN	WOOTTON J	M	GREY	A	O			O			O	O		O	O	O	
SEN	JENNINGS A	M	GREY	A	O			O			O	O		O		O	
NA	DICKINSON K	M	GREY	A	O	O		O			O	O		O		O	

O – OFF
C – AWAY ON A COURSE
L – LEAVE DAYS

leave key entry for all 700 nurses. Although work patterns have changed, the computer, to a large extent, replaces a manual system by an electronic one.

The computer does impose better discipline by requiring that information about courses and the re-allocation of nurses to wards, shifts or leave should (ideally) be available before a new schedule is produced. (Changes can be made later but this is less efficient). Apart from details of a few courses and a handful of staff there are no operational reasons why most of this information should not be available, but it still requires clarification of procedures and responsibilities. The rest of the system and its wider benefits depend on attention to this seemingly minor detail.

(d) *Day sheets*
Day sheets contain a list of all the nurses working on that day by the six-week schedule. They also contain a supplementary list of nurses on courses, staff sick and staff on middle days (for possible overtime call-up). An example is shown in Table 7.4. To this sheet is added, alongside the nurses involved, both routine ward duties and special duties. The computer produces a basic day sheet for each

Table 7.3 Typical shift patterns

FILE 51 SHIFT CYCLES   UPDATED 5/12/83

NO. <--42 DAY-CYCLE BEGINNING SUNDAY----->

NO.	S	M	T	W	T	F	S	S	M	T	W	T	F	S	S	M	T	W	T	F	S	S	M	T	W	T	F	S	S	M	T	W	T	F	S	S	M	T	W	T	F	S
B6						O	O	O						O	O	O							O	O							O	O							O	O		
B7	O						O	O	O							O	O							O	O							O	O							O	O	
N1				O	O	O						O	O	O	O					O	O	O	O					O	O	O	O						O	O	O			
N2			O	O	O						O	O	O						O	O	O	O					O	O	O	O					O	O	O					
N3		O	O	O						O	O	O						O	O	O						O	O	O	O					O	O	O	O					
N4	O	O	O						O	O	O						O	O	O						O	O	O					O	O	O	O					O	O	O
N5	O	O					O	O	O	O						O	O	O						O	O	O						O	O	O						O	O	O
N6	O					O	O	O	O					O	O	O	O						O	O	O					O	O	O						O	O	O		
P1	E	E	D	D	O	O	E	E	D	D	O	O	E	E	D	D	O	O	E	E	D	D	O	O	E	E	D	D	O	O	E	E	D	D	O	O	E	E	D	D	O	O

O = OFF
D = DAY SHIFT
E = EVENING SHIFT

Table 7.4 Section from a day sheet

13/10 83 DAY SHEET FOR MENTAL ILLNESS DIVISION			
NAME	A.M. DUTIES	P.M. DUTIES	EVENING DUTIES
GREY WARD 007			
SN SMITH M			
SN ASHTON P			
SN WILLIAMS AP			
SEN SCOTT P			
NA JONES P			
RED WARD 005			
CN HILL C			
SN WOOTTON J			
SN FARRELL P			
SEN JENNINGS A			
NA DICKINSON K			
PINK WARD 005			
CN DAWES J			
SN MOORE H			
SN PATEL B			
SEN TURNER A			
GREEN WARD 002			
SN HAWKINS K			
SEN CHAPPELL K			

SPECIAL DUTIES			
CN ROSE H	ESCORT ANYTOWN 2.30		
SN BRISTOLL C	ESCORT ANYTOWN 2.30		

FIRE PARTY			
CN BARKER L			
CN DRIFTER M			

Division automatically (and sheets up to 3 days ahead). All the list writing and typing is thus computerized.

(e) *Overtime records*
Special duties and the completion of manning requirements may involve overtime for nurses not originally scheduled to work. This overtime is noted on the day sheets. Payment is arranged at the end of each monthly

period from a further sheet recording for each day of that period, the hours, if any, for each nurse.

The computer stores all this information and eliminates the need to log overtime on a second sheet. The calculations are done automatically and, of course, perfectly. At the end of a period the computer prints a list of staff and overtime. Reasons for overtime can also be logged as an easy adjunct to logging the hours and since the data are stored in the computer it can be analysed with little effort as shown in Table 7.5. A summary of overtime is produced for hospital records and senior nursing officers.

In addition to these principal features of the system, computer programs have also been implemented to deal with nurses on maternity leave, budgetary control of nursing expenditure, amendments to the Mental Health Act 1983 and patient admissions, transfers and discharges.

Management and systems issues

(a) Optimal versus sub-optimal efficiency

The problem of sub-optimal efficiency which arose when each SNO pursued his own procedure has largely been removed as a consensus has been achieved on the appropriate system. However, this change has undermined some of the power of the SNOs and transferred it to the Allocation Officers who understand better how to run the system. A transfer of power has also arisen as a new SNO, responsible for administering allocations, has been appointed. The lines of responsibility and accountability between the SNOs and the Allocation Officers have thus become blurred.

(b) Resources released

The computer has taken over most of the clerical work of two people who worked below the Allocation Officers. This saving of time more than pays for the computer and in theory releases the nurses concerned for other tasks. In

Table 7.5 Overtime analysis

MENTAL ILLNESS DIVISION

OTHER DUTIES OVERTIME   JANUARY 1 TO FEBRUARY 1

DATE	NURSING OFFICER	REASON	CHARGE NURSE	REASON	STAFF NURSE	REASON	S.S.E.N.	REASON	S.E.N.	REASON	N.A.	REASON	TOTAL HOURS
01/01/84			8.50	N.O. DUTY									8.50
01/01/84			4.50	V.P.									4.50
01/01/84					11.00	LODGE							11.00
02/01/84			12.50	LODGE									12.50
02/01/84					11.00	LODGE							11.00
02/01/84			5.00	N.O. DUTY									5.00
03/01/84	8.50	N.O. DUTY											8.50
03/01/84					14.75	HOSP. ESC.							14.75
04/01/84									14.75	HOSP. ESC.			14.75
04/01/84	0.75	ALLOCATION											0.75
04/01/84									11.00	LODGE			11.00
05/01/84			12.00	ESC/HOME									12.00
05/01/84									12.00	ESC/HOME			12.00

practice, however, one of them is used by the SNOs as a liaison officer with the Allocations Officers.

(c) *Aggregated information as a management tool*
One important feature of the information provided to the Chief Nursing Officer is an overtime report. In a time of severe budget constraints in the NHS such a report may provide some insights into where savings may be made. However, at present the managerial use of this information, and of other aggregation reports that could be provided is not well developed. To some extent this may be attributable to the general underdevelopment of the line management (as opposed to administration) function in the NHS and an emphasis upon consensus management. In the Hospital, consensus management involves the three Chief Officers (Figure 7.4). In addition, a certain level of overtime has become institutionalized as part of normal expected salary and its removal poses serious employee relations issues.

(d) *General administration function*
An SNO Administration has been introduced into the Nursing Division, which itself purchased the computer system. The possibility of conflict and duplication with the Administration Division has not yet been examined. This reinforces the point made earlier that line management in the NHS is in general weak. The integration of systems across functions (nursing, medical, administration) is severely hampered by this weakness. Although the Körner Report has proposed such an integration, it is questionable whether it can be achieved unless the Griffiths proposals are successfully implemented. It is perhaps not entirely accidental that the system discussed here and that reported by Verguillas have involved the nursing profession, which traditionally has had a well-defined authority structure.

(e) *Resistance to change*

The resistance to change aroused was limited by the after-math of the crisis referred to earlier. The Committee of Enquiry which investigated the state of affairs at the hospital recommended that, amongst other things, a com-puterized work-scheduling system be introduced. There was, therefore, a willingness to co-operate which may not otherwise have been there. The outside consultant, the agent of change, was able to benefit from this atmosphere. When outside consultants come into an organization, unless the change is fundamentally sound, the organization may well revert to the old ways of working when they leave. The system is still running at the time of writing which indi-cates its fundamental soundness.

However, some resistance did materialize after the system was implemented, mainly as a result of the impli-cations of the SNO's power-base being eroded as much control passed to the officer running the system. Attempts had been made at the outset to make the SNOs aware of the implications of the impending change. Their reaction was to send themselves on a computer-programming course rather than to face the organizational issues. The resistance took the form of complaints about inflexibility, which asserted incorrectly that the six-week schedules could not be changed once the computer had produced them and about the maintenance of subordinate personnel or tasks which were no longer necessary but had been components of some power-base.

Conclusions

This chapter addressed the introduction of computerized working scheduling systems in a 'not-for-profit' organiza-tion. It discussed the problems in effecting such a change in an organizational structure as seriously constrained as the NHS. Four important and interdependent recommendations emerge: first, line authority is required, particularly for integrated systems; second, a leader or agent of change is needed to push through and maintain the momentum of change, reinforced by line authority; third, to minimize resistance (and given previous developments in the NHS) collaboration must be encouraged; fourth, in such inert systems, change is best implemented against a background of crisis or turbulent conditions.

References

G. Bevan et al., Health Care Priorities and Management, Croom Helm, 1980.

DHSS, Health Services Management: Implementation of the NHS Management Inquiry Report, London, DHSS, June 1984.

H. Elcock and S. C. Haywood, The Centre Cannot Hold: Accountability and Control in the NHS, pp. 53–62.

R. Griffiths, 'NHS Management Inquiry', London, DHSS, 1983.

S. Halpern, 'Question Time for Griffiths', Health and Social Service J., p. 696, 14 June 1984.

S. Harrison, 'Consensus Decision-Making in the National Health Service—A Review', J. Management Studies, Vol. 19, No. 4, pp. 377–94, 1982.

S. C. Haywood and A. M. Alaszewski, 'The Outcome of NHS Reorganisation: Structural Change and Implementation of Social Policy', Public Administration, pp. 37–51, 1979.

D. J. Hunter, 'NHS Management: Is Griffiths the Last Quick Fit', Public Administration, Spring, pp. 91–4, 1984.

R. Klein, 'Performance, Evaluation and the NHS: A Case Study in Conceptual Perplexity and Organisational Complexity', Public Administration, Vol. 60, Winter, pp. 385–407, 1982.

J. G. March, 'Footnotes to Organisational Change', Administrative Science Quarterly, December 1981.

R. Maxwell, 'International Health Comparisons: What Can They Tell Us?', Public Money, March, pp. 35–40, 1984.

D. Miller, 'Evolution and Revolution: A Quantum View of Structural Change in Organisations', J. Management Studies, Vol. 19, No. 2, 1982.

D. J. Rhodes, M. Wright and M. Jarrett, 'A Simple Diagnostic Tool for Identifying Weaknesses in Small Manufacturing Control Systems', Proceedings of the Inst. Elec. Eng., 1982.

D. J. Rhodes, M. Wright and M. Jarrett, *Computers, Information and Manufacturing Systems*, Holt, Reinhart and Winston, 1984.

C. Snyder *et al*., 'Designing a Quality Assurance Information System for a Process Firm', *J. of Engineering Costs and Production Economics*, April 1985.

M. Verguillas *et al*., 'Standard Nursing Information Package for Planning, Evaluating and Training (SNIPPET)', *North Western Regional Health Authority*, 1984.

M. Wright, D. J. Rhodes and M. Jarrett, 'Growth, Survival and Control in Small Manufacturing Systems', *European J. Operational Research*, Vol. 14, No. 1, pp. 40–51, September 1983.

M. Wright and J. Coyne, *Management Buy Outs*, Croom-Helm, 1985.

8 Prospects for the 1990s

Introduction

In 1977, a large steel company implemented an 8-bit, micro-computer with 250-kbyte disc drives and a 48-kbyte memory. It was used to monitor orders as they passed from the order-book through the various stages of production in the rolling and finishing processes. The computer cost £8,000 and comfortably handled the application for nearly one thousand orders and up to one hundred items of information per order. One man kept the system up to date each morning, that is during half his working day, using data from all over the works. At weekly intervals, over a period of 3 hours, the computer produced reports: list of arrears, load on capacity, order intake and production output, analysis by value, product type and market sector. These were used by the production controller, the sales, mill and finishing process managers, and the finance and managing directors.

In 1985 most manufacturing companies have not managed to computerize their operational activities to anything like this extent, even though some have had access to mainframe computers for years, and all may now buy microcomputers of at least five times the speed and capacity of that above, for less than half the price.

Despite the interest in word processing, very few government offices, with all the bureaucratic and clerical effort that their work involves, have moved beyond the telephone and copying machine, so far as IT is concerned. The 2,623 robots (December 1984) in the United Kingdom are fewer than the numbers in use among the country's industrial competitors, notably Japan (64,600), the United States

(13,000) and West Germany (6,600) and at approximately 1 robot per 25,000 people are a mere fraction of the potential. Despite the air of excitement, only a fraction of the potential has been realized.

As Nolan observed (Chapter 4), exploitation generally lags far behind the opportunities and as this book has demonstrated, the effective use of IT in organizations is surrounded by difficult issues. The biggest change during the next ten years is going to be simply the more widespread use of IT, with the majority of companies doing what a minority do already. Much of the impact will be concerned with the scale of change, with exploiting the means of transmitting and processing data through a more efficient and effective infrastructure. A much smaller number of companies will nevertheless be pioneering the newer ideas and products about to emerge.

As we have seen in Chapter 2, the change involved in the adoption of IT is influenced by factors both external and internal to an organization. External factors were seen to relate to both supply and demand. It is possible to predict what might happen in IT between now and the 1990s, based on a knowledge of existing technology. However, adoption of new IT will be effectively determined by whether the demand exists in the market-place to support it and whether an organization is equipped to assimilate it.

This chapter begins by discussing what is likely to be available; firstly, presenting a view of technology as it might affect organizations and secondly, illustrating expert systems, a new idea which in the longer term will have a profound effect on people, particularly managers. The influences of demand factors in the market-place and managerial factors internal to the firm are then examined in an attempt to identify problems which are likely to be encountered in the widespread adoption of new techniques.

The four main aspects of IT identified in Chapter 1 continue to be relevant. Display and storage technology should improve in quality and fall in price but communications and processing power, including software, are likely to be the key to changes over the next few years. Communications have barely been exploited and processing power continues to lag behind the theoretical concepts already available. The major industrial countries have all followed Japan's lead in investing heavily in IT and the United States is reported to be now investing more money than the Japanese are in computers and related fields. The British Government has already invested £570 million and is committed to the collaborative European ESPRIT programme and their own ALVEY project. IT is being taken seriously but it remains to be seen whether governments can manage such ambitious projects successfully. Unless a particular company is directly involved with one of the projects they are unlikely to benefit for several years yet. However, the projects cover all aspects of IT, not just computers, so specialist companies must stay alert to the possibility of sudden developments. Communications is a particularly significant area with far-reaching possibilities, implications for competitiveness and new business.

Communications

The means of separately transmitting pictures, voice or data signals between any two places on (or off) Earth has been available for many years as the transmissions from any space mission will confirm. It is, therefore, possible to conceive and implement any configuration of interconnected computers, satellites, television cameras, data links, storage devices, facsimile machines, television sets or radios. Unfortunately, the cost would be very high because there is no single network even at a national level to handle the many users and various types of information involved. It would be very difficult to obtain a single network, partly for technical reasons: (i) Television (picture or image) transmission requires much higher rates of information flow than radio or telephone and has historically used different equipment and communication channels. Telephone trunk lines have to handle many separate channels simultaneously so their full capacity is, in any case, not available to any one user.

(ii) Television, radio and voice transmission are, however, mostly transmitted using similar analogue techniques (continuous signals at varying frequencies) and the information processing they require has been limited to the two conversions; image or sound to signal for transmission and signal to image or sound at reception. No intermediate manipulation of the information, such as checking the syntax of a sentence, has hitherto been necessary. Computers, in contrast, communicate by digital rather than analogue methods. They not only manipulate information, but actually exist to do so. Processing data has been their forte. Nowadays they are being developed to process speech and images as well, manipulation is essential at almost all stages and this means using digital techniques.

Large systems need to handle more than one user per channel simultaneously. Communications in IT systems concerned with data, text and images, that is, most future systems, thus depend on the development of techniques to handle many forms of information quickly and in a convenient and compatible way. High-speed transmission of primarily digitized information is likely to meet the requirements and several manufacturers in various countries already have suitable systems to offer. However, there are further complications, this time political and economic.

Firstly, to be effective the communications networks and general infrastructure should be at least national and preferably international in scale. This raises issues of national interest because if the United Kingdom, for example, were to choose a foreign system it would put indigenous manufacturers of IT equipment at a disadvantage.

Secondly, telephone networks in the United Kingdom and most other countries which already have telephones, have a major investment in the existing circuits which enter almost all buildings and extend for hundreds of thousands of miles. These circuits (coaxial cables) are estimated to represent 40 per cent of the total cost of the entire telephone system. They are only suitable for relatively slow rates of digital transmission (1,200 characters per channel per second) because they were designed for speech not data or images. However, in the past few years optical fibres have been developed, which provide a superior means of transmission. They are more efficient and cheaper than coaxial cable, particularly suitable for high transmission rates over long distances and not vulnerable to interference from lightning and other circuits. Beyond 1985, British Telecom has decided to buy no more coaxial cable, but the recent developments in single-mode fibres and stable, semiconductor lasers will ensure that the fibre-optic possibilities continue to present new opportunities to the policy makers. The above developments, for example, increase the light that emerges at the end of a fibre and reduce the need for the repeaters usually spaced along the length of a cable to maintain a healthy signal. It may be possible to operate up to 100 km without repeaters; in which case the United Kingdom network could operate without a single repeater at a considerable cost benefit. British Telecom plan to have 50 per cent of their trunk network on optical fibre by 1990. Beyond 1990, it is expected that transmission rates twice as great as the 565 Mbit/s (all channels) currently being specified for optical fibre systems will be achieved. This will permit image transfer by digital means at a quality similar to the current television pictures.

So there is a need to balance caution and bravery. Installing a new infrastructure too soon could hasten obsolescence and commercial difficulties might follow. Waiting too long could be equally catastrophic because competitors who were more positive would fill the gap. Part of the answer seems to lie in the establishment of technical standards. Both customers and suppliers can use standards to

measure their requirements or judge their opportunities.
Standards can be hammered out by knowledgeable parties
before significant resources are committed. Standards can
be announced well ahead. Standards provide some form of
stability in a rapidly changing field, but they can also be
regressive, restrictive and technically inept.

Open Systems Interconnection (OSI) is the standard
favoured by the UK. The OSI model is being drawn up by
the International Organization for Standardization. The
idea is that all equipment should be able to communicate
easily, regardless of manufactuer. Open Systems Interconnection will offer a set of standards covering everything
from the number of pins on a plug to the way computer programs work together. Eventually these standards will be
divided into seven groups, or layers, each corresponding to
a different level of communication.

Systems Network Architecture (SNA) is the IBM
standard. It offers fewer options than OSI at present.
Because of the commercial and political implications, and
since there is competition from British Telecom, it is both
unlikely and undesirable that it should dominate the
British market.

Progress in communications over the next 10 years is
thus going to be more dogged than exciting, involving the
installation of optical fibre cables and associated terminal
equipment at a rate determined largely by British Telecom
and demand from the market-place for improved performance. Since the demand will depend on suppliers producing IT equipment which meets that performance there is
something of the chicken-and-egg about the situation.
Good and widely accepted standards should reduce the
problem and allow suppliers to design, and invest in, speculative products. Meanwhile, the trends are to exploit, on the
one hand, the existing infrastructure as much as possible
and, on the other to develop stand-alone IT products which
will eventually act as a spring boards to exploit those future
opportunities.

Exploiting the existing communications infrastructure

In the national/public domain the existing telephone network offers links which, though originally designed for speech, will handle data at rates of up to 1,200 characters per second per channel and are widely used. Packet Switching (PSS) was introduced in 1982 to operate as a parallel network, but dedicated to data alone. This allows automatic routing of packets of data from one site/installation to another by the most efficient route. It is currently being integrated with the existing public telephone network to increase its catchment area. Third parties can make use of this network to provide what are becoming known as Value-Added Network services (VAN). Chang, of the Butler Cox Foundation, defines a VAN as follows:

> There are essentially three components: the first, is that it is telecommunications-network based, the second, that there are third parties involved, and the third, value must be added on top of normal voice and data. The third-party element comes in because, if a large organization uses a network to communicate with its own divisions, no matter how big, no matter how complex, that is not a VAN. However, if the same company uses a network to communicate with either its customers, its suppliers, or its peers, then that could be a VAN depending on what they do with it, and what they do with it must be to add value.

Networks currently operating or in the development stage can be divided up into three categories:

- those offering processing and information storage to a wide spectrum of users, such as electronic-mail services;
- those providing specific services to industrial or commercial groups such as Nottingham Building Society's Homelink company-to-customer system;

- those operated by very large database owners to publish information.

In the first category, British Telecom Gold is an example of an electronic mail service which operates over national and international public telephone and data networks, and is accessed by dialling a number on the telephone, connecting the receiver to a terminal, via a modem, and keying in a password. The service provides:

- Instant dispatch of messages with simultaneous distribution to several destinations;
- Shared information files for processing or access by a chosen group of users;
- Password-protected company information;
- Access to telecommunications facilities, such as telex, radiopaging and telemessaging.

Messages can be filed then retrieved by subject, keywords, date, sender or recipient using practically any approved terminal. Also, text can be generated offline using a word processor and then connected to the service when required. Costs for the service are based on the period of connection at standard or cheap rates in the United Kingdom, or number or characters sent outside the United Kingdom.

In the second category, services for industrial or commercial groups include such things as home banking, airline reservations and travel services. Several companies already provide VANs to cover these sectors and many more are in the development stage. Homelink, from the Nottingham Building Society, is an example of a 'small' concern taking advantage of the new technology.

Homelink joins the customer to the Nottingham Building Society, the Bank of Scotland and a range of shopping services via an ordinary television set and a console, supplied by the society. The system is operational for eighteen hours a day, seven days a week and enables the customer to view an account statement, transfer funds between bank and building society or vice versa, apply for a mortgage, obtain a loan quotation, make holiday reservations and armchair shop at discount prices. Basic Computing Services Ltd. offers a reservation system for tour operators known as Holidaymaster. The system is easy to operate, and enables travel agents to have direct access to the tour operators' computerized brochures. The agent can use the system to make an inquiry, get a quotation, make a booking, amend it or cancel it, and there is no danger of unauthorized access as every agent is given an agent's number or password. A full booking list can be displayed giving the date of booking, date of departure, number of passengers, destination and the cost of the holiday, and a warning facility is available to enable tour operators to indicate price changes or brochure errors. Holidaymaster costs include an initial registration fee, which includes consultancy and training, a terminal maintenance fee and an annual licence fee. After these have been paid, the service is costed on passenger volume.

Cable & Wireless plc has recently set up an electronic mail service aimed at the small businessman. Known as Easylink, the service enables users to send and receive telexes and desk-to-desk electronic messages at the office or at home, and is available to anyone who has access to a telephone and a microcomputer or word processor. To transmit a message, the user prepares the text and rings the Easylink number. The system asks which type of terminal is being used, requiring a two-digit code to be entered, then asks for an identity number and password. If the identity number and password are correct, the system will accept the message and send it to the destination chosen. It will also retry an engaged number if required.

In the third category are the companies offering a facility rather than a specific service, e.g. selling the capacity of a category-two, type system for other companies or individuals to use. A good example is Prestel, offered by British

Telecom. This uses the idea called videotext (originally called viewdata*) because its principal function is to display and modify text. Information is stored in a central computer as a series of frames or pages. The beauty of the system lies in the simplicity of use which is independent of information content. Any kind of information can be stored or retrieved. The disadvantage is that it may be difficult to find the required information which is stored by page number, although using one 'page' as an index helps avoid major difficulties. Users buy capacity on the system and the right to access restricted and confidential parts of the database. Financial centres like the City of London are exploiting this kind of facility and 600 more terminals were installed for city dealers in the period 1982–4. Overall more than two million Teletext terminals are in use in the United Kingdom.

Developing IT possibilities aside from the infrastructure

Because of its comprehensive network of interconnections in homes, offices, factories and stores, the telephone system is the future basis for IT communications generally. But, while the telephone utility companies are organizing their networks much scope remains for stand-alone equipment and independent systems.

At the home and in the office, computers can be connected at low speed with the telephone network as already described. Locally they may be interconnected via high-speed lines which are an integral part of the computer system. Local Area Networks (LAN) exploit this possibility.

* Viewdata should not be confused with Teletext, a system for transmitting 'frames' of information using normal television broadcasting techniques. Teletext is a one-way system with a limited number of frames (a few hundred) being transmitted in sequence and the receiver has to wait for the required page to appear.

An example is shown in Figure 8.1. Note the gateway for potential connections to external communication networks. They have some advantages over centralized systems and are being marketed by all major computer manufacturers:

- they provide distributed computing power which may be used independently by the local user;
- they provide access to common data and to data from other users;
- they allow expensive items like data-storage units and high-speed printers to be located in one place without depriving users of access to them;
- they do not commit a company to a large system at the outset because they can be extended as training, understanding and investment allow;
- if properly managed, they reduce the likelihood of duplicating data and inefficient file maintenance;

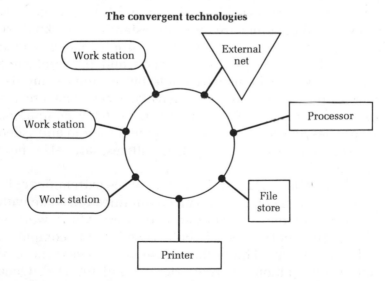

The convergent technologies

Figure 8.1 Local area network

- they impose on all users some uniformity of standards and procedures;
- technical and training skills are transferrable within the one system.

Excluding for a moment the many areas of manufacturing and process technology, such as machine tools and robots, which do not present problems of communication *per se*, the main areas for independent development are, of course, computers. Microcomputer development continues apace and in high technology companies high-resolution graphical displays have displaced drawing boards and are being used for the preparation of drawings and circuit diagrams. Television studios use equipment, such as that supplied by Quantel, which will digitize the analogue image from the television cameras and manipulate it digitally. The manipulated data is then reconstituted into analogue form for transmission as usual. The insets, overlays, enhancements, zooms and tumbling, kaleidoscopic tricks regularly featured in television programmes are all produced in this way. Electronic games manufacturers are also interested in these kinds of techniques because they want to supply games which have both television quality displays and the interactive possibilities that the usually crude but exciting computer games already possess. High-density, laser discs are the result of this kind of development. Portable computers, telephones and offices, even a scheme for audio and video conferencing between dispersed offices, are also now available.

Naturally the tools and techniques at the extremities of IT systems are less concerned with communications than with the power of the hardware and software. Much work is being carried out on speech, both as an input to computers and as an output. The problems are nevertheless those of pattern recognition, analysis, storage and retrieval. Once speech is mastered synthetically, keyboards, displays and printers will be less critical in the 'man-machine' interface as this aspect of IT is often called.

Processing power

Engineers and scientists identify four generations of computers up to and including those of the present day. All are based on the von Neumann principle which, in short, uses a central processing unit to carry out instructions one at a time, *sequentially*. In 1981, Japan announced a plan to develop what are now known as fifth-generation computer systems. These, apart from being even more powerful, will be distinguished from other generations by their use of a non-von Neumann principle. They will have processors which carry out many instructions simultaneously, that is in *parallel*. The plan recognizes that by the time such machines (computers) are available it should be possible to use speech to communicate with them and that many of the techniques of artificial intelligence (AI), expert systems (ES) and logical programming could be embodied in the new designs as shown in Figure 8.2. Many of these ideas are thus included under the umbrella term 'fifth generation' as well.

To explain a parallel-processing computer requires at the outset, a reasonable understanding of sequential, von Neumann machines; a task outside the scope or purpose of this book and probably beyond the immediate interest of the reader. The essential distinctions between the two kinds of computer can, however, be illustrated by analogy.

Assume that you are firstly a sequential-type of processor. You are instructed by a program for the purpose of this illustration to build a house (rather than to manipulate data or codes as in a real situation). Your every move is determined by the program:

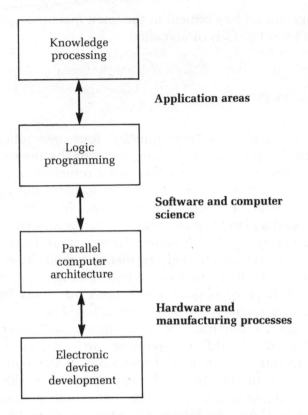

Figure 8.2 Fifth-generation computer project

—— fetch shovel, dig foundation 1, dig foundation 2, dig foundation 3, fetch sand, fetch cement, fetch water, mix sand with the water and cement, fetch a brick from pile A, place a brick on wall 1, etc.

It may of course be more convenient to do the foundations 1 and build wall 1, before digging foundation 2, but you will never have the opportunity to find out because you must obey the instructions according to the sequence in which they are written.

Now imagine yourself as a parallel processor. This is difficult because you are a 'singular' person. Therefore, consider yourself and your extended family to fit the role instead. This is easier and more analogous to the actual processor. Your cousins can fetch the shovels and your nephews dig all the foundations while you fetch the sand. Your children can mix the cement while your brother organizes the bricks. Mum can build wall 1 and sister wall 2, etc. all at the same time.

In this second case, the way the instructions are formulated must, of course, be different from the first to obtain full benefit from the approach. This is a very important further distinction and advantage of parallel processing. It has tremendous implications for software development and the kinds of computer language to be used in future. For a sequential computer program instructions are carried out in order, 1, 2, 3, 4, etc. In parallel, processing instructions are carried out as soon as the conditions are right. This is when all the data they need are available, normally upon completion of some other instructions. In the above analogy, the instruction, build wall 1, could occur when the foundations 1, bricks and cement were complete; that is regardless of the state of foundations 2 or the whereabouts of the shovel. So, in a parallel machine with a suitable program, instructions are carried out according to general progress not according to a fixed sequence. The greater the progress, the faster the program.

A practical example in data processing would be the search for a thousand different items in a large database. A conventional computer would require a thousand separate searches one after the other. In a parallel-processing computer, the thousand could in principle be sought simultaneously at an obvious saving in time.

Fifth generation is thus a well-defined engineering goal with less well defined, but tantalizing software possibilities. There are already logic programming languages like PROLOG and LISP, which, although running on sequential computers at present, really require parallel processing to exploit their full potential. PROLOG is, in fact, likely to be the core language of fifth-generation machines.

Yesterday we spoke of 'data processing' (DP), today we speak of 'information technology' (IT). Tomorrow it is likely to be 'intelligent knowledge based systems' (IKBS). The term is used in the name of an Alvey sub-program, and 'knowledge base' and 'knowledge engineer' are creeping into computer jargon particularly in the growth area of expert systems. These are examples of IKBS and though only for use on sequential computers at present, they are sufficiently effective to provide a modest taste of more remarkable things to come.

Of the various expert systems developed, MYCIN is one of the oldest and most interesting. It was developed at Stanford University in the United States to provide consultative advice on the diagnosis and treatment of infectious diseases. This was regarded as a useful area on which to concentrate, as a general physician is not always fully conversant with all the vagaries of such complaints, yet prompt action is needed to fight the infection. In formal clinical evaluations MYCIN has been found to compare favourably with expert consultant physicians, not only in the identification of the pathogen but also in diagnosing treatment and averting overprescriptions. This is especially meritorious, as the standard clinical approach has been to prescribe a broad-base antibiotic treatment that can lead to harmful patient reactions, and the development of drug-resistant bacterial strains.

Apart from its use as a diagnostic tool, MYCIN has subsequently been developed for a number of other applications. It was stripped of its application-specific knowledge, leaving the inference structure called EMYCIN (empty MYCIN). The adapatability of EMYCIN as a knowledge-handling system was then tested with a problem encountered by a software house marketing a library of structural-analysis programs for engineers. The software house had found that the whole package was so complex that users often took over a year to become proficient in using the program library. EMYCIN was used to build an expert system to guide the user through the library. In addition, MYCIN was in frequent use by medical students because the orderly arrangement of knowledge made it more useful than an ordinary textbook. This was explored by Clancey at Stanford. He added 200 additional rules to MYCIN to create GUIDON. This steers the dialogue with the medical students in a useful way, presents diagnostic strategies and constructs a student model.

The domain of expertise of operational expert systems is not limited to the field of medical diagnosis. The identification of molecular structure is important to a wide range of problems in chemistry, biology and medicine. Often sophisticated X-ray crystallography is not practicable or available, so researchers have to interpret other data, such as those obtained from mass spectrometers, to derive theoretically possible structures. This is the purpose of DENDRAL, which identifies the possible molecular structures that could account for the spectroscopic analysis.

As well as chemical analysis, synthesis is also important, especially for the development of new drugs, and ascertaining how drug structure relates to biological activity. This is the specialist area of the SECS (simulation and evaluation of chemical synthesis) system, an organic synthesis program written at the University of California. SECS and the similar systems, LHASA and SYNCHEM have already proved useful. One expert has been quoted as saying that DENDRAL and SECS have as much reasoning power as most graduate students.

Another successfully developed expert system, PRO-SPECTOR, is used in the field of hard-rock mineral exploitation. PROSPECTOR has performed satisfactorily when ascertaining the likelihood of certain minerals being present in regions of interest. One of the more interesting trials was made in 1982, when PROSPECTOR and a group of geologists were given the same field study data about a region in Washington State. The system predicted that there were appreciable molybdenum deposits in the area, while

while the geologists said that this was not the case. Subsequent mining of the area confirmed that PROSPECTOR was correct. The system is currently in service with the US Department of Energy and the US Geological Survey.

On this side of the Atlantic, the SAGE system was announced in May 1982. ICL is using SAGE for projects associated with the introduction of its new mainframe range later this year, while Shell has used SAGE to build a political risk system. ICL is using SAGE to assist with the development of a design and consulting aid to examine pipe cracking. BHRA is using the system to gauge flow rates and patterns in pipes.

The importance of such systems in defence-related uses should also be noted. It has been reported that the Pentagon's Defense Advanced Research Projects Agency is providing research into artificial intelligence as a whole with a budget of approximately $1 billion, and has already announced plans to use expert systems in satellite control systems that will reason, plan and navigate.

This is an impressive list of applications though little appears to distinguish these systems from many others that do not claim to be 'expert'. Indeed a commonly agreed definition of an expert system has not yet emerged. However, the following components would seem to be necessary:

a knowledge base;
an inference engine;
a user interface.

The inference engine is where parallel-processing, fifth-generation computers will make an impact and promote really powerful expert systems. Inference is currently handled by programs in sequential machines and because of the relatively slow processing there is a limit to the size of system worth practical consideration. Inference and knowledge are the essence of expert systems and it is necessary to examine what they are and how they are related to appreciate the fundamental ideas.

In a conventional computer system, any data-processing application for example, the program and data are easily distinguished as in Figure 8.3(a). Without reference to any documentation (or the program itself) the data would appear as a meaningless series of numerals and characters [e.g. 1191, 67, 15, R. HANBURY, V128, 17, 12, 84]. However,

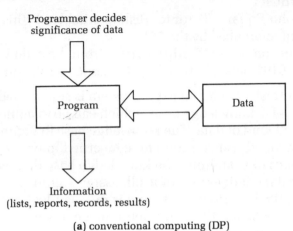

Programmer decides
significance of data

Program ⟷ Data

Information
(lists, reports, records, results)

(a) conventional computing (DP)

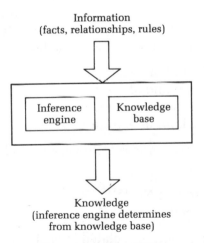

Information
(facts, relationships, rules)

| Inference engine | Knowledge base |

Knowledge
(inference engine determines
from knowledge base)

(b) expert systems (IKBS)

Figure 8.3 Conventional and knowledge-based systems

the program would have been written with foreknowledge of what significance the data should have. The program, because *it knows*, can thus tell us when printing some report or other, that the above line means:

Order Number 1191 of 17th December 1984 for HANBURY
16 Soho Square, Toronto, Bishop Auckland (this from a record referenced by the 15)
Product on order: Wardrobes (this from the code V128)
Price £197.56 each (this from the codes V128 and the R).

In contrast, data for an expert system is superseded by the concept of a 'knowledge base', which can be imagined as an enhanced kind of data. The knowledge base in Figure 8.3(b) is maintained via a program concerned more with the mechanics of examining the knowledge base than with the specific data. It does not, of itself, assign significance to the items in the knowledge base and is independent of the particular knowledge therein. Such a mechanism is the principal element in programs referred to as expert systems' shells, of which SAGE and EMYCIN are examples.

A knowledge base will normally contain symbolic representations rather than numbers or isolated items of text. One type of knowledge is *facts*, such as:

potato is a kind of vegetable
vegetable is a kind of food
food is a kind of sustenance
Norfolk is a kind of garden

Another type concerns *relationships*, such as:

Jill needs sustenance
potatoes grow in Norfolk
Jill lives in Norfolk

in which some facts are related to each other to increase the amount of meaning. To actually reason, it is further necessary to introduce *rules* or conditional relationships. These provide the basis for inference, for solving problems or making decisions. Examples of rules are:

if Jill lives in Norfolk
and Jill needs sustenance *and* Norfolk is a kind of garden
then Jill plants potatoes

The answer to the question 'Does Jill plant potatoes?' would elicit the answer 'yes' from the small example knowledge base above, because the inference engine will reach that conclusion by a self-directed search.

The better systems have a friendly interface with the user. This provides scope for a dialogue, asking for information which will help to fire rules, suggested by the knowledge the system already has, and giving lists or explanations of the facts, relationships and rules encountered during searching. Broadly, this is how all current systems operate, although there are a number of variations that confuse the uninitiated. These variations need careful consideration before one attempts to implement a system, but in themselves are matters of detail.

Firstly, there are the logical computer languages favoured by workers in the field of artificial intelligence and expert systems. It is possible to write an expert-system program from scratch in these languages and computer scientists often do so. Languages like PROLOG, POPLOG and LISP are in this category. This approach is very fundamental, akin to writing a bespoke program for a conventional computer application, and should not be confused with buying an expert-system shell, which is akin to buying a conventional package. Shells are, of course, empty of knowledge initially. They can be written in many languages; FORTRAN, PASCAL, PROLOG and LISP have been used among others.

Secondly, there are different types of inference mechanism. They are distinguished as 'data driven' or 'goal driven'. In the data-driven method, all the items relevant to a given problem are examined to see which rules they fire. These rules then provide a new set of items which, on examination, fire further rules, and so on. Eventually a small number of items, singular conclusion or diagnosis is reached.

The goal-driven method starts with a hypothetical conclusion and checks to see which rules and conditions need to apply for it to be satisfied. Each sub-condition spawns a further set of rules/conditions to be checked. If the checks can be completed the initial goal is deemed to be satisfied.

Thirdly, there is the treatment of uncertainty. Real experts judge that certain events, diagnoses or lines of action are correct, not on the basis of absolute certainty but on the grounds of reasonable probability. When assembling a knowledge base, some expert systems make provision for rules to contain probability weightings, e.g.

> if the patient has a sore back
> *and* has fair skin
> *and* has been sunbathing
> *and* has no other symptoms
> *then* it is *90 per cent certain that* the patient has sunburn.

When many such rules are used the probability of the outcomes are assessed using the Bayesian method of combining probability. Outcomes are, in these systems, given a certainty factor to guide the user as to the strength of the advice.

Developments in expert systems

The main constraint on expert systems at present is the writing down of knowledge in an explicit way suitable for use. To do this requires great skill and the co-operation of an expert. Those capable of formalizing knowledge are mostly *not* experts in the area of concern, they are computer scientists, engineers and other intellectuals drawn to the field of expert systems and not experts in the areas of potential applications. They are referred to as knowledge engineers or system builders and appear to have a distinct role at the interface between the true expert and the intended system. It is hard to believe that systems will propagate very rapidly if such skilled people are necessary, but in the medium term they are essential to what is really a learning process. Until sufficient experience has been built up about the methods of extracting and formalizing expertise there is little chance of simplifying the knowledge engineers' tasks into techniques for easy assimilation and widespread use. One of the obstacles is that experts are frequently unable to explain how they use their knowledge; they just do. Therefore much work has yet to be done on the formation of knowledge. Meanwhile, the very process of thinking about the rules which govern expertise in the many areas of application appears to be beneficial, whether or not a system is implemented. Even if parallel-processing computers were already freely available they would, for these reasons, have no immediate impact. However, as these difficulties are removed the limited power of sequential machines will eventually become the main constraint. For the moment, £600 will buy an expert system shell for a microcomputer. As people experiment with this kind of tool, the valuable experience needed to exploit the systems to come in 5 to 10 years time will begin to accumulate.

In the context of this book, one looks to expert systems to help with the management of organizations and, in particular, to improve the management of manufacturing industry. The potential is considerable and the rewards for success likely to be high, but getting started is difficult. First attempts can easily arouse unduly high expectations with subsequent disappointment, disillusionment and rejection of the idea. Also, managers are not, in the main, people who lightly divulge the reasons behind their actions.

Nevertheless the case for expert systems to support decisions is strong because they are:

- able to cope with subjective rules and contingency factors (which mathematical methods do not do);
- advisory, the user can still use his own judgement;
- likely to be consistent under similar circumstances, a feature which though not necessarily optimal may provide stability and predictability, both of which bolster confidence;
- an explicit statement of what is often inaccessible, stored in someone's head (this means that experience does not leave with the personnel who acquire it);
- capable of storing the collective wisdom of all interested parties which is likely to be better than that of one (possibly biased) individual;
- able to give a view virtually instantaneously (experts are primarily distinguished from other able people by this feature).

In common with human experts they can, of course, offer the wrong advice occasionally and are only as good as the knowledge fed into them.

The following is an example of how an expert system can be set up to support management decisions, in this case at the operations level in a steel company. The items are illustrative, not definitive, and one must stress that it is the views of those knowledgeable about the area of concern that count. A discussion like this is only a guide as to what sorts of facts, relationships and rules might be used. The particular facts, rules etc. are a matter for the managers involved.

Figure 8.4 shows the kind of information structure required. The commitments of the company, such as the order-book, are planned in the light of available capacity and the policy (aims) of the company. As plans are carried out transaction data records progress. In a practical IT system all this activity is noted in a database which should therefore contain the operational status of the company in information terms. Reports are obtained from this kind of database to provide management information. They represent the current state of the art as regards decision support. However, an expert system of the type discussed above may be inserted as shown. The knowledge base for it has three ingredients:

1. What is the range of decisions in the area of interest? For example, 'What should the mill do next?' A set of possible decisions is shown in Table 8.1 (the 'don't know' decision, not included here, is sometimes valuable to complete the set).

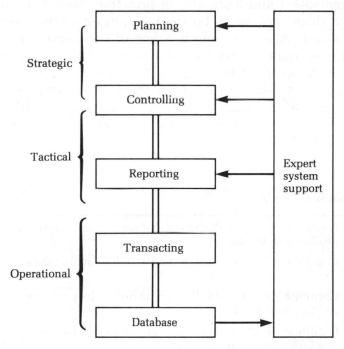

Figure 8.4 Information structure with supporting expert system

2. What are the factors in the area of concern which seem to bear upon the decision? Table 8.2 gives a simple, illustrative set of factors, or attributes as they are termed in expert-system jargon. A practical set would be larger and might also include financial values (profit, cost, contribution) and factors to indicate inconvenience or preferences. It is expected that the values of the attributes at the time a decision is made will be explicitly available from the database.

3. What rules relate the decisions of 1 to the attributes of 2 and in particular how are they influenced by their values?

Ingredients 1 and 2 should, in principle, pose little difficulty since they must be used in any other method of decision-making. For safety, a few of the more marginal attributes and rare decisions may be included. Some expertise is none the less required to define attributes and decisions and either an expert or committee must make the selection. More skill is required to sort out the rules of ingredient 3 in order to enter the knowledge into an expert system shell.

Table 8.1 Decisions

C1	Continue rolling with the current section and largest order available in tonnes.
C2	Continue rolling and roll the next orders by due date sequence.
C3	Continue rolling and roll the next orders by customer priority sequence.
C4	Continue rolling and roll next orders in due date sequence (excluding overdue orders).
C5	Change rolls to next section.

Table 8.2 Attributes

	ATTRIBUTES		N-ARY
TASK	LENGTH OF ORDERBOOK IN WEEKS		0 1 2 3 4 5 6
	TOTAL WEEKS OF CURRENT SECTION ON ORDER		0 1 2 3
EFFECTIVENESS	WEEKS OF OVERDUES CURRENT SECTION BEING ROLLED		0 1 2 3
	CLASS A CUSTOMER ORDERS PRESENT		Yes No
EFFICIENCY	AVERAGE ROLL CHANGES PER WEEK		0 1 2 3 4
	NEAREST VALUE OF RELATIVE SECTION EFFICIENCY %		20 50 80 100 120 150 180

Rule induction is a technique which may help here. It is a method of discerning the minimum number of rules which satisfy a given training set of attributes, values and decisions. Table 8.3 is a small set of different, but typical combinations of attribute values and the decision an expert feels is appropriate. The expert could be the production controller or mill manager, that is someone who normally makes the decisions anyway. A practical set might well contain several hundred lines or instances as each example is called. On the assumption that the training set is representative, the rule induction technique reduces the set to a smaller one which covers all cases. These rules can be expressed as a decision tree as in Figure 8.5. The rules are basically similar:

if attribute A_1 has value V_1
and attribute A_2 has value V_2
and attribute A_3 has value V_3
then make decision C.

If a situation should arise that is not covered by any rule the answer is NULL or 'no information available to advise a decision'.

Whether or not rule induction is used, the combination of attributes, rules and associated decisions are intrinsically suitable for a knowledge base. A particular set can be modified with the benefit of experience or as policy changes. There is nothing to prevent a manager ignoring the advice that the system recommends and there is every prospect that the thinking through of the rules and careful maintenance of the knowledge base will improve understanding of the decisions being taken.

The market-place and the organization

The adoption of the above developments in future will depend on sufficient demand existing in the market-place

Table 8.3 Training set

TRAINING SET

Order Total ≤3≡0 >3≡1	Section Total ≤1≡0 >1≡1	Section Overdue ≤1≡0 >1≡1	Class A Customers? No≡0 Yes≡1	Rolls per Week ≤3≡0 >3≡1	Section (Relative) Efficiency ≤1≡0 >1≡1	Class
*	*	1	0	1	*	C1
*	*	1	1	1	*	C3
*	0	0	0	1	*	C4
*	1	0	0	1	*	C2
*	*	0	0	0	1	C5
1	0	*	0	0	*	C5
1	0	0	1	*	*	C3

TASK   EFFECTIVENESS   EFFICIENCY

* A 'don't know' condition

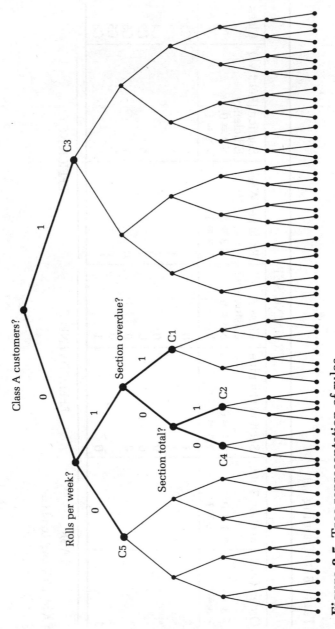

Figure 8.5 Tree representation of rules

and the ability of the internal arrangements of organizations to assimilate such developments.

A direct way of assessing the likely impact of IT is to survey the views of organizations which might adopt it, and this is particularly useful where the aim is to meet demand in the market-place and to improve efficiency of internal management. We are able to report the results of a survey of the likely impact of IT in the personal financial services market, carried out by one of the present authors, and of a survey of the use of IT in production management carried out by Muhlemann et al.

The survey of institutions operating in the personal financial services market was carried out in early 1985, and the important results for our purposes are reported in Table 8.4. Four major conclusions may be drawn from the table.

First, IT is expected to have an important influence on their business, between now and 1990. This is agreed by the

Table 8.4 The expected impact of IT in personal financial services market by 1990

	Very important %	Important %	Unimportant %
Communications with customers	43	45	12
Communications with agents or other institutions	47	40	13
Developments of new products	44	45	11
Cost saving	45	48	7
Use of databases	43	48	9
'Paperless' office systems	18	56	26
Improved M.I.S.	51	43	6
Element of growth strategy	33	54	13
Constraint on growth	10	48	42
Encouragement of growth	24	56	20
Base for percentages = 212			

Source: Mike Wright and Trevor Watkins, 'Survey of Trends in the UK Personal Financial Services Sector', *Nottingham Institute of Financial Studies*, 1985.

overwhelming majority of respondents, including even those who do not envisage that it will be a major influence in their growth strategy.

Second, IT is expected to have a major influence on the efficiency with which business is controlled and with which it is conducted. Respondents gave the greatest weight to improved management information systems. Cost savings and communications links are also expected to be important by the great majority of respondents.

Third, the impact of 'paperless' office systems is seen as far less significant in general.

Fourth, a significant proportion of companies expect IT to have a major influence on achievement of their growth plans. But, over half of respondents see IT as being an important factor constraining their growth. The unease could be accounted for by at least two reasons: either, the belief that technology and its acceptance will not keep pace with the plans of the company; or, the fear that those companies left behind, or making the wrong choices, during a period of rapid change will suffer. On the other hand, some 80 per cent of respondents see IT as encouraging growth.

Two major areas where IT may make a contribution are home banking and the electronic transfer of funds at the point of sale (EFTPOS), as we have seen in the previous section. However, although the technology is essentially available, there are question marks over likely adoption in the near future. In the United Kingdom, the penetration into the market of Prestel has been quite low, despite the very high level of penetration of home computers. The Nottingham Building Society had a very specific motive for its introduction of Homelink—an economic alternative to opening new branches on a national scale for a fairly small regional society. Although the number of Homelink subscribers cannot available, the low number of Prestel subscribers suggests it cannot be very high. To date, the Nottingham Building Society scheme has not been emulated by others, although a number of banks are experimenting with similar schemes. In the United States developmental activity has gone further, with Chemical Bank in New York probably being one of the leaders. However, the introduction of the scheme has been far slower than anticipated with major revisions being required to meet consumers' needs. Moreover, current penetration is limited to a very affluent end of the market—it is not a mass-market product. Hence, those organizations that wait-and-see may reap more benefits than those first in the field. The respondents to the survey were not very optimistic for a high penetration of home-banking facilities in the next 5 years. Only one-third thought it would account for over 5 per cent of personal financial transactions by 1990.

As regards EFTPOS, it has been argued that it can only become economically viable if it is competitive with cash, cheques or credit cards and that this is unlikely to happen. EFTPOS may offer security over cash, but the low cost of using cheques/credit cards and the benefits to be derived from the delay in debiting of accounts may make it unattractive to the consumer. Indeed a Consumers' Association survey reported that 58 per cent of respondents did not want EFTPOS.

On the other hand, the development of automatic cash dispensers (ATMs) has recently proceeded rapidly, being introduced as a means of reducing the cost of money withdrawals from banks and being accepted by customers not least because of its 24-hour availability. Although mainly of the in-the-wall form, there has more recently been a return to their provision within branch lobbies. The reason for this switch is the marketing potential of the bank lobby where the customer can possibly be sold a range of banking products.

Other benefits of IT identified by respondents in the personal financial services sector, and reported in Table 8.4, concern business efficiency both within an organization and in its communications or transactions with other organizations. This has implications for the way in which institutions providing personal financial services diversify into new product areas with the relaxation of regulatory constraints. In the 1960s and 1970s such diversification would most likely have been by creation of a conglomerate concern through acquisitions. Studies of this process have revealed that serious managerial problems arise because of a lack of expertise in managing certain product areas. A preferable alternative is diversification through joint ventures, which provide the benefits of individual organizations' expertise in certain areas as well as new products. Joint provision of the necessary infrastructure/network may be required to obtain economies of scale where an individual organization cannot afford the entire cost.

One of the major benefits of the recent generations of IT is, as has already been noted, its lower cost and hence enhanced accessibility to smaller companies. The survey by Muhlemann et al. examined the adoption of IT for various aspects of production management in companies with fewer than 450 employees. The results of this survey are summarized in Table 8.5. Over 40 per cent of the 364 respondents were found to use IT for some application, with stock control being the most prevalent. In other areas, such as planning and scheduling, IT was used in relatively few cases even though respondents admitted that these activities consumed a significant amount of time. In a high proportion of cases, the use of IT had not even been considered, though for production planning, IT was under consideration in almost half the companies. In very few instances had IT been tried and abandoned, whilst there was significant evidence that IT had been considered and rejected for certain applications. The reasons for rejection were quite varied, but in order of decreasing importance, the major ones were: the problem was thought not big enough to warrant IT; cost; potential changeover problems from manual systems to IT; fear of purchasing incorrect equipment. In respect of cost, it was felt that the investment in IT should pay for itself through cost savings within

Table 8.5 IT and production management in smaller companies

Application	Percentage of respondents stating that				
	Computer used	of those not using a computer, its use			
		is being considered	has been considered and rejected	has been tried and abandoned	has not been considered
Raw material stock control	24.4	52.1	14.6	2.7	30.6
Time/cost estimating	19.8	43.0	12.2	1.8	43.0
Materials estimating	14.2	34.6	11.8	1.3	52.3
Production planning	13.3	47.2	11.5	1.3	40.0
Analysis of delays/performance	9.0	28.3	8.7	0.4	62.6
Analysis of breakdowns	3.5	16.0	8.4	0.4	75.2
Maintenance planning/scheduling	2.1	14.9	8.3	0.4	76.3
Quality control	4.7	21.9	7.5	0.4	69.2

Base number of respondents = 364

Source: A. P. Muhlemann et al., 'The Application of Microcomputers in Production Management', OMEGA, Vol. 12, No. 3, 1984, pp. 321–5.

12 months, which is perhaps optimistic where no significant clerical savings are available. Even so, there was generally improved control as a result of the introduction of IT. The importance of collaboration in the introduction of IT was clear in over half of the cases of implementation, with team membership being generally comprised of computer supplier, managing director, production manager and external consultant.

The importance of top management commitment to the project was thus evident. There is, however, an important distinction between top management's commitment and their direct involvement in the project. It is necessary to ask what important tasks top managers are not doing when they are involved in detailed system design.

These two surveys indicate growing adoption of IT in different business circumstances, but also areas where IT may not be appropriate or where adoption appears sluggish in view of its potential. Market conditions may make a particular development inappropriate, or its introduction may be delayed because of cultural lags in the market. Internal managerial factors also influence the rate at which IT developments are adopted. As the survey shows, managers expectations of what IT can do, in terms of both cost-savings and capabilities, must be realistic. But, in the potentially important area of integration of activities, the organization's ability to reconcile what may be conflicting demands of different departments is more significant than advances in the power of IT. This is not a simple problem, and there are dangers in the taking of short-cuts. Each organization needs to pursue a route which will deal with its own particular circumstances. This book has proposed a methodology by which organizations can do this. Organizational learning is a key element in managing the introduction of IT. Different organizations learn in different ways. However, certain general prerequisites for the learning involved in the introduction of IT emerge from the theoretical and case study material presented here. Assuming the technology exists and that environmental conditions warrant its adoption, there is a need for an agent of change who is responsible for achieving change within a given period of time. This agent of change may be an 'enthusiast' within the organization or an outside consultant. Often the agent's role will be taken by both these people. The agent requires senior management support and authority to make changes, as well as the co-operation of those affected. Fear and ignorance of change, often expressed as refusal to acknowlege its necessity, resistance to its implementation or unrealistic expectations about its capabilities, may be the major impediments preventing organizations from progressing far enough up the learning curve to exploit IT successfully. The existence of the technology and the expected developments in the next 10 years mean that for those companies which can deal with the internal problems of introducing IT, and which can correctly identify the opportunities, the rewards are there for the taking.

References

J. L. Alty and M. J. Coombs, *Expert Systems—Concepts and Examples*, NCC Publications, 1984.

D. Michie, *Expert Systems in the Micro-Electronic Age*, Edinburgh University Press, 1979.

T. Moto-Oka (ed.), 'Fifth-Generation Computer Systems', *Proceedings of International Conference in Tokyo*, North Holland, 1982.

G. Moore, 'Value-Added Network Services', *Electronics and Power*, IEE, January 1985.

A. M. Starrs, 'Expert Systems—Their Uses and Possible Impact on Society', *Electronics and Power*, IEE, January 1985.

B. Wilson, C. C. Berg and D. French (eds.), *Efficiency of Manufacturing Systems*, Plenum, 1983.

Index

(NOTE: *passim* means that the subject so annotated is referred to in scattered passages throughout these pages of text.)